FOREWORD

According to my personal experience and understanding, this project would be most effective for an individual (with some sort of self-awareness and consciousness) seeking an intimate relationship, companionship and partnership/already in an intimate relationship, partnership/marriage, and are genuinely willing to (individually, and together with another) submit and surrender to the unseen forces which govern this seen reality we physically exist in. This project is for one who doesn't desire to be manipulated and controlled solely by their thoughts, emotions, and feelings, for one who chooses not to be trapped inside of the body and the body's-workings, for one who seeks the existence of a connection, and/infusion of a union or possible androgenous reality and experience beyond the human shell and human behavior we animate as.

This is not your traditional "book"/"manual", I don't necessarily consider myself an "author"/"writer", I'm just an individual having an interesting experience within the silence and privacy of my own mind and my own perception that I'd like to openly share/publicly share to unknown but chosen listeners, not only verbally but in written-form as well, basically in as many ways and as many avenues as possible, on any platform/platforms the energy and or spirit chooses to express itself on and express itself through. For a while I wanted to put out a book/project of some sort based on this personal realization within this specific experience and understanding, but it didn't come to surface, and I didn't understand why, until my awareness informed me of/revealed to me the fact that I was still in the middle within and living through the very reality I was currently writing about, which in other words were implying that I couldn't close a chapter of my life that was still in progress and still an on-going concurrent thing in my reality. I eventually settled with that realization and kept on experiencing the very thing I was ready to write about, maintained my center, remained patient, and moved accordingly.

What I eventually came to realize, that my 'calling' in this life (or that which silently and privately speaks to me and through me in my mind and spirit throughout this reality and experience) was based on the acknowledgment, experience, and understanding of what 'Principle'/'Principality is', and to exist/live moment to moment within it and throughout it.

WHAT WAS THE BOOK WRITTEN FOR? WHY NOW IN THIS SPECIFIC TIME AND ERA?

I felt this book needed to be written in this specific moment and time (with me simply as a messenger or conduit) for the awareness and realization of ones deeply hidden emotions, feelings, thoughts, and moods, with the assistance of stillness and silence (in the moment of a potential confrontation/friction), for the control and discipline of one's deeply subconscious destructive hidden emotions, feelings, thoughts, and moods, to pull them up to the surface of the conscious mind, in order to be addressed and mutualized by the awareness, control, and discipline of ones being, through the given pathways of both mind and body. Individual's hearts, organs and bodily energy-fields are deeply disturbed, interrupted, saturated, and drowned in emotions, feelings, repetitious thoughts and reoccurring moods, empowering itself with memory, imagination, and absence of presence and unawareness of moment, due to a loss of knowledge of it.

WHY PRINCIPLES?

To supervise, monitor, and manage your feelings, emotions, and thoughts (in order to steer them and convert them into a tool towards your own clarity and sanity), as they occur spontaneously and unpredictably, subconsciously. And as you consciously supervise, monitor, and manage these subconscious-trainings in a silent centered space of patience, observance and awareness, a respectful distance and space creates and appears instantly between you and them, between your reality and that truth of existence, which in contrast, are two parallel existences in synchronicity with each other. It's about giving another an opportunity to experience their own inherent-divine freedom, for a chance/possibility of self-liberation, due to a lot of personality-bashing and ego-colliding between male and female parties. Now what happens when the platform for the personality is no longer there as a battleground for potential conflict?

Biological and psychological neutralization, and energy mutualization.

Be principle before personality. As you interact and embrace each other as principle, a new personality will begin to grow from that interplay and interaction. Let the structure/structuring of a personality grow and/sprout from the foundation of principality.

WHY IS THE INFORMATION IN THIS BOOK NEEDED NOW?

Well, before I explain further, let's take a look at some facts. Based on 'Abuse' (both verbally and mostly physically) there are 750,000 'Divorces' annually in the U.S.A., also, according to NCADV.org/National Statistics, more than 10 million Men and Women go through 'Domestic Violence' annually in the U.S.A., and according to UNODC/United Nations on Drugs and Crime, 6 out of 10 'Murders' are 'Women', which basically means half of all murdered women are killed by intimate partners. It's no question why there are more than 50.000 'Marriage Therapists' in the U.S.A.

So, to make a long story short, to sum this up into a simple understanding, we have become too 'Personal', not only with ourselves, but with others as well, significant others, to be exact and precise. Where is our acknowledgment, knowledge of, understanding, and applying of the law of 'Principle' in our intimate relationships? I recommend one to incorporate it within that specific atmosphere of experience, why? Because it is your intimate partner (along with family and family members as well) who you are 'Mentally' and 'Emotionally' connected to and connected with, and those who we are mentally and emotionally connected to and connected with have the most influential affect on our mentality, feelings, and emotional-body, which means they possess the ultimate influence of our 'Triggers' and trigger-like nature towards them, and towards ourselves. Feelings and emotions are a given, an obvious thing, and it's not about focusing on those given aspects of life because they're going to be regardless, this path is about acknowledging and focusing your attention on the most subtle and subliminal aspects of life, which is known as principle, and to become principle in almost all of your doings and beingness, to animate as it, act as it, and express yourself as it. With this practice, you have to first harness some kind of Self-'Control' and 'Discipline' of self, along with the principles of 'Patience' and 'Consideration' for yourself, and for your other. Once this occurs you will immediately become witness to a new possibility of yourself unfolding and revealing itself to you and before you. Remain aware to the revealing.

WHO AND WHAT REALLY IS THIS BEING THAT I CALL MY "Partner", "Companion", "Significant-other", "Girlfriend/Boyfriend", "Lady/Gentleman", "Woman/Man", "Wife/Husband"?...

Well, to be "quite frank" and to get straight to the centered point from a metaphysical and occult point of viewing... the who and what you call these names are just…

- **Company** (just something around you, around your orbit, around your cypher)

- **Something around you that can come and go, appear, and disappear** (a thing which you are not glued to chained to stuck to or conjoined with, a thing has legs, a thing which possesses will, ability, prerogative, opportunity, choice, and decision, inside of a place which has doors and windows that can open and close, surrounded by an inside and outside reality just like you)

- **A projection you created** (unconsciously, subconsciously and/consciously. Your eyes are your own personal projector, which project outward what the slides of the mind create inward, connected to the energy chemistry and biological chemistry of your deepest feelings, needs wants and desires, a depth which you see and know, and a depth beyond what you see and know, but are and always were)

- **Your personal creation** (with its own experience and its own free will. We are creators)

- **A "figment of your imagination"** (something which once existed in your imagination. Something you once imagined would become true)

- **A physicalized-fantasy, which derived from an unphysical-reality** (something which developed within the blueprinting/traced-connected points-of-reference of your mind and feeling. A thing which once was a

deep desire you possessed/which is a desire you still possess)

- **The outside-experience of your inside-existence** (an outside "them" of an inside you. Your internal energy, feelings, needs, wants, desires, and fantasies projected outward as an external animation you're your external reality to interact with, in order to activate your internal purpose)

- **Another 'You'** (which is outside of your you-self, to physically interact with. The word another is the word 'An'– 'Other', which is implying that you are here in this reality by yourself)

- **A specific 'embodiment' of your 'mental' and 'emotional' focus** (where mind goes energy flows, and where energy flows an entity grows, and soon shows)

- **A magic trick you did** (you're a magician by nature. Your birth is magic)

- **The "rabbit out of the hat" trick** (an Extremity [Rabid] of Track of mind [Trick] that has arrived and became a physicalized-energy-sort)

- An external fulfiller for certain voids you personally internally possess
(we're governed within the principles of void and fulfillment)

- **A 'voice', 'presence', and 'movement' in your peripheral vision** (just a functioning thing in operation mode)

- **A 'desire'/certain desires** (a thing embodied within one unit/one orbiting representation, in presentation of a physical form, in compliment to your physical form, because ultimately it is you that you are standing in front of and with)

- **A 'need' in physical form** (that which is felt will be formed)

- **A 'want' in physical form** (that which you seek will be seen)

- **An 'example' of your magic speaking back to you** (a confirmation that your 1 dimensional 'intent' transformed into an 'actualized' thing in 3rddensity. From a flat plane of existence into a pop-up plane of experience)

- **The 'confirmation' and 'validation' of you being a 'magician'** (something created by you and given to you within your own inherited divine right, because there is nothing outside of you)

- **The '3-D' example of your '1-D' mental and physiological activity** (as above so below, as within so without)

- **A 'participant' with potential to 'volunteer'** (there's no separation, only distinction and personal experiences)

- **A 'phenomenal-reflection' of the 'phenomenon-projecting'** (You being the thing which is projecting)

- **A 'possibility', with 'equal-possibility' to become "impossible"** (A present thing, with potential to become a past-thing. A present experience, with potential to become memory. Every projection has its own device of choice and decision, to stay or leave)

- **A 'challenge'/'self-challenge'** (an outside animation to interact with, in order to initiate and inside activation)

- **An 'inside-thing' appearing as an 'outside-thing'** (if they truly existed on the outside of you, then how are they affecting the inside of you?)

- **A 'test'** (a challenge of self that you've created for yourself, for your divine purpose)

- **An 'ability' and 'opportunity'** (a lesson you've created for yourself, knowingly and or unknowingly)

- **The complimented-polarity** (a physically-interactive-polarity of yourself)

- **Another 'yourself' keeping 'itself' company** (it's all just you. Nothing is outside of you and never was outside of you. What we know as outside and inside are an illusion that is being experienced and witnessed by you, the creator of it all)

- **A mirror** (a frame in your mind/mirroring reflection, reflecting a 3-D image that you can touch and physically interact with, which was created from a 1-dimensional platform of intent)

- **A factor** (a factoring of 'self-mastery')

- **The principle of 'Desire' and' Possession'** (what is hidden internally, shall reveal itself externally)

Hello, my name is Blu, I am currently writing my first book based on the metaphysical understanding of relationship, partnership, and companionship. I attended a university in 2010 for metaphysical psychology, and currently being enrolled in college for human behavioral science, a.k.a. human behavioral psychology. I have always had a natural interest for the workings of the mind in the union and play of human-to-human interaction. It fascinated me to see the counteracting intelligence of mind-to-mind intra-action, the giving-taking receiving-delivering reciprocating actions of 2 or more lives at play, so this is the path in my life at this very moment in my life that was simultaneously chosen by me and given to me. I always found myself somewhat indifferent from peers I had around me or found around me and stuck out in crowds for that reason, based on how I thought and how I perceived life according to how it was revealing itself to me or unraveling before me. In sharing my thoughts and perception with others I found there were not too many individuals I was relating with or were in relation to what I was sharing, so in that interaction and feedback it inevitably and eventually made me go deeper within myself and my own unique understandings. I eventually came into my own calling of who and what I was in this moment of space and time in life and proceeded in this direction, a direction that inevitably led me into this specific point of focus. Welcome.

FOR ANY QUESTIONS/FEEDBACK CONTACT ME BY EMAIL AT
Asulazul11@gmail.com

INTRO

THINGS TO 'KEEP IN MIND AND HEART' (K.I.M.A.H.)

Throughout the Book/Manual you will see at the end of each section five initials such as 'K.I.M.A.H.', which stands for 'Keep In Mind And Heart', meaning 'keep these statements, explanations and elaborations in your mind and in your heart as you move throughout your experience, as a navigating tool to reach the ultimate destination of clarity and sanity for mental and emotional balance, in order to carry out your divine mission and spiritual purpose with least distractions and interferences (created primarily by you) while remaining on your path.

The purpose of these points I touch upon throughout this project, is to recede you back to a zero state of being, and to function from that specific platform of 'beingness' within the reality of 'doings' or 'doingness'. As you 'do', never forget how to 'be'.

The whole point of this book is to bring about immediate 'Realization' within one's mind, reality, and perception, from the source-point of awareness acknowledging an undeniable truth, in order to drop or suspend the "personality" aspect of one's experience, in order to see and acknowledge the existence of 'Principle', and its subtle and subliminal purpose within the very middle of our physical and non-physical experience and existence.

- You are in this whole experience completely by yourself (who else is in your mind but you?)

- You projected a partner through your personal and private needs, wants, and desires (this reality is based on the principles of 'Void' and 'Fulfillment', wherever a void appears, a fulfillment arises. Every 'calling' gets 'answered').

- The self-projected-partner appeared as an 'effect' (an effect that is a reflection as a 'cause' of 'you')

- The projected-partner appeared so that you can interact with them through principles/through the medium of their principality through the surface of their "personality", for the sole purpose of spirit enhancing itself (spiritual infusion), using the devices of image, body and personality for communication, connection and interaction, to return to its individual uniting of self, through the illusional reunion of its "split" (spirit uses/utilizes the physical functions for its divine operation)

- Since they're created from you, projected from you, for you, they're indefinitely going to reflect things, ways, behaviors, interests and characteristics of you, because they are you (what you call "having things in common"/"having the same interests")

- Only you can keep yourself company (Not "someone else"/"anyone else", because what you call "someone else"/"anyone else" does not exist. Decode and decipher your interactions with "others"/"another")

- The primary and ultimate Being that you are is spirit. Which is the alpha and omega of your reality\reality itself

- Spirit is selfish (meaning 'Self-less')

- Spirit can only see itself (nothing else can exist in its view but itself because nothing else besides itself exist)

- Spirit can only be with itself (spirit is not "quantity", it is 'Quality')

- According to spirit nothing else is in existence but IT

- Spirit cannot be "split" (it's an entity of 'multitude' existence)

- Spirit is only here to unify itself/imbue itself (there's no such thing as "you met her"/"she met you", that's all just spirit unitizing itself through the illusional-vehicles of you and "another")

- Only 1 (spirit/"love") can hold 2 together ("people"). Only glue/a paper clip/a staple can hold two pieces of paper together. In other words, find out what the glue, paper clip and staple is, what it represents and stands for (spiritually). Without a 'middle' there is no existence of "sides".

Contents

Section 1

WORSHIP

If you find yourself worshipping something that you don't necessarily choose to

worship, then that means you're possessed "So how do I come out of that

possession?"

The action taken to create space from it "What is the action I need to?"

The chemistry of action starts as an intent, then a biological effect, then turns

into a physical/kinetic action "What do you mean by this statement?"

Which emotions and thought forms have the strongest hold on you? "Why?"

Be aware of what levels of the body and what locations within the body that you

become enslaved to, serve, and begin to follow "Why?"

Whatever emotions and thought that control the way you think and act, are the

very things you work for and work under "What do you mean by this

statement?"

You are possessed by it "Possessed by what exactly?"

You become possessed by this energy "How?"

You can consciously/unconsciously create your own pull/pulling "How does this

happen?"

The more you unknowingly worship an energy, the more stronger it gets "Why

does this energy move in that way?"

Everything outside is just a hologram of what the inside is projecting outward

"How is this so?"

To shake you up in a way and make its way to the surface of you and your

awareness "Why?"

Neutralize it "In the example of a conflicting relationship triggering me

emotionally, how do I go about neutralizing that?"

Every source unto itself seeks its own resource "Meaning what exactly?" We're

beings that direct our attention with reason "Meaning what exactly?"

It is you feeling those specific feelings, not them "So how do I balance out that

understanding within myself at the moment of interaction?"

Worship has nothing to do with expecting in return "Why can't I expect

anything in return?"

The self which Is permanent "What's the permanent thing that I am?"

Worship what the feel is like "Meaning what?"

A mutual harmony of silence within yourself "Describe that mutual harmony of

silence that forms inside me once I acknowledge principle"

You were born with slaves/servants/things that already worship you and serve

you "What are these things?"

WORSHIP (K. I. M. A. H)

Section 2

STATUES

You don't always need something/someone to listen to your thoughts and mental

dialogue "Why?"

It's also helpful to possibly see their physical representations as well "What

physical representations?"

You need things to stare at around you without those things noticing you staring

at them "Why so?"

By something not playing back/interacting back with you, you get to have a clear

and private space for self-reflection "And what do I get in return?"

A statue is a status "And how does status relate to this understanding?"

You reflect that which you come in contact with "Meaning what?"

Statues are still things that speak to you and through you in silence and presence

"How so?"

Interacting with something in complete silence opens up the mind's and expands

its vastness "And what happens from this?"

Finding/recognizing the principles within an individual makes you respect them

as a god-like figure " And what does this mean?"

Let that god-like force navigate itself in whatever direction it chooses to " And

what comes about from this?"

STATUES (K. I. M. A. H)

Section 3

EMBRACE DISLIKE

Dislike equates to space and distance "In what way?"

The action of self-involvement is an automatic effect "Due to what exactly?"

Learn to respect principle itself "What does respecting principle mean?"

Dislike is just as important and relevant as closure "How so?... explain please"

There's no logical need to hate principle "Why?"

Embracing dislike is respecting and enhancing the principles of expression "How

so?"

Within your ignorance/unknowing, all you're really seeking in another is

territory and property, not freedom and respect "How would you know?"

To dislike, is to create space from another "So what should I do?"

Dislike can also assist in a respectful release "How so?"

Don't become to neither like nor dislike "Ok, so what should I do then?"

You are composed of two complimentary existences, a left-brain hemisphere and

right-brain hemisphere "Besides what I'm composed of, where does the I exist

within this understanding?"

With sharp awareness, you slide a very short distance "Which means what?"

The outer signs you can visibly identify "What do these visible identifications

represent?"

EMBRACE DISLIKE (K. I. M. A. H)

Section 4

COMMUNICATION AND EXPRESSION

Section 5

TREAT/TRICK

It's not ultimately about treating an individual a certain way, it's more about

being aware "How do I do this?"

Section 6

LIVE/LOVE

The best thing one can do for another is to keep them live, which is to

acknowledge them and give them attention "What is attention?"

What is the point of having life around you, if you don't acknowledge the life

which is living around you? "Why do plants grow when you're singing to

them/are around them?"

Section 7

KNOWING AND FEELING

Even when one is describing their feelings to you, they themselves may not be

describing it to a 'T' "Why not?"

Section 8

I OF YOU

I love. "Why did he reply like that? What does that mean?"

'I of you', is the same thing as saying 'I am of you' "How so? In what way?"

Section 9

LOVE AND LIKE

Section 10

LOVE SONGS

Most so called "love songs" have addictive and obsessive lyrics within it "Hmm..

interesting. How so?"

They all at some point throughout their songs repeat these 7 words "So what

happens if I repeat these same 7 words while I'm singing?"

The more we consciously repeat these words, the more they echo throughout our

skull and brain "What happens in the brain during these echoing of words?"

Section 11

GLUE

Every relationship is based on a gluing of some sort
"Meaning what?"

Me meet to join, we join to bond, we bond to bind
"Meaning what exactly?"

There's different energy forms of bondage/bonding
"How so?"

The mind and body has devices to glue you to itself
"Like what?"

Section 12

MAGICIAN

You draw things up, then draw things to you "Why is that? How is that?"

These are things/vacuum-like energies that pull in outside realities "Can you

give me an example?"

What we know as the past and the future can only be born from the present

moment "Which means what exactly?"

This is something to understand "What do you mean by that?"

The time-vehicle (the body and brain) is directly connected to your

time environment "So what am I?"

Whatever you really want and/feel the need to be, that is a force that remains

devoted at your feet awaiting your command and demand to manifest itself

"Why does that happen?"

You are a thing which draws things up from a 1-dimensional plane of existence

"Give me an example please"

Magic just means to make things happen out of a nowhere "How often does that

happen?"

You can manifest things into 3rd magnitude from 1st cursory "How so?"

Your magic is a transforming stage that goes from feeling into touch "How and

why does this happen?"

The body is not just a body, it's a magical manifesting machine "What do you

mean by a magical manifesting machine?"

SUMMARY

Book written by AMIAS ASIAM

RELEVANT INFORMATION IN REFERENCE TO THE PURPOSE OF THIS PROJECT

Let's take a look at the catalogue of thoughts that roam around in our brain when we are possessed by our created identity and personality. These are the thoughts that occur when one is their lower nature of jealousy, ownership, possession, and insecurity, these are the thoughts (along with feelings to match the vibration of the thought being held in place and or reoccurrence) that carousel in the brain during certain situations that happen within an intimate relationship, when one is feeling unsure and or uncomfortable about something, due to their own possessive nature and insecurity.

Keep in mind as well that these are same reoccurring thoughts that appear every time in every intimate relationship you're in/every intimate relationship you find yourself in, with different individuals at different times in your life, so instead of thinking that it's the other person which is causing the problems, one may find it wise to possibly ask their self (accompanied by common sense), "are these thoughts even real?". The evidence of this truth is the constant reoccurrence of the exact same dialogue throughout totally different experiences with different individuals. How is it possible to have the same exact dialogue within different experiences and different interactions? A question one may want to ask their self (with awareness, consciousness, common sense, logic, silence, stillness and fairness) before they enter into another possible intimate relationship or while they're in a current intimate relationship now.

Where are they going?

Why are they wearing that outside?

Who are they talking to on the phone?

Who else are they talking to while I'm on the phone with them?

Who's calling them right now?

Who are they texting?

Who's texting them?

That's showing a little more skin than usual.

Who are they dressing for and trying to impress?

Why haven't they called or text me yet?

Where are they at?

Who are they with?

Are they with someone else?

They're lying to me.

Oh, they think I'm stupid? Ok.

Who's making them smile and laugh like that over the phone and on the laptop?

They don't laugh like that with me.

Why are they so happy all of a sudden?

They said they were just going to the store and back, it's been over 2 hours already.

These questions create another personality out of you, and soon develops into a certain kind of unharmful behavior that has potential to become a violent behavior (depending on one's awareness, patience, control, and discipline of self, throughout the momentary possession that's presently taking place between time and space). Be aware of the same reoccurring questions that carousel and cycle throughout the brain, potentially influencing you to act-out those specific thought patterns by any means necessary for perceived necessary means for identity-justification and egoistical-satisfaction (two things that were created by you and your experience, that possess no true divine source of existence).

Instead of thinking thoughts in that self-destructive dialogue to self, counteract it with immediate focus on self and one's own beingness and doings, so for example, instead of saying to yourself silently/verbally "what is she doing?", counteract it with a silent dialogue to self saying "what am I doing today?", instead of saying "where is she/where is he?" say "where am I? and what am I about?", practicing with this formula of mind will keep the immediate focus on self, encouraging self-progress and magnifying self enhancement. Do this technique genuinely, not with intentions of being opposite and doing opposite of your destructive thought, the main things/truths which assists with this method of thinking and being are the following: genuine self-interest (really being interested in yourself, both spiritually and physically), knowledge to know that you're in this whole experience by yourself, knowing that your mate is your own personal creation that you created (knowing they're not outside of you, and that they're actually inside of you. An energy turned entity), knowing that nothing in this physical experience is real including your physical body and the brains experience, knowing that you're not from here and that you're only currently projected here at the moment, knowing that you only exist within a moment, knowing that what we know as time is an illusion, knowing that your divine existence is separate from the body's experience, not caring about the things you usually care about, knowing that you're just here to collect experiences that do not belong to you but belong to the body, knowing your just a composition of principles, and knowing this present body and brain isn't yours, never was yours, and never can be yours (it's just a machine and device to use and utilize for navigational purposes for an unknown but divine purpose beyond the physical body and its physical internals). Keeping all these things in mind and heart (K.I.M.A.H) throughout your intimate relationship experiences, gives you a kind of constant freedom from the present experience being experienced by you, when the freedom, release, space or gap between you and another is desired/required by you, for whatever reason.

To make a long story short/a short story long, take from this practice what you will, whatever you find relative and relevant to you and your understanding and interpretation of this personal path and it's correspondence to your private calling in life. Never deny what's silently talking to you and through you. Be the truth that you are, but most importantly, the truth that is you.

AS YOU ARE.

WORSHIP (Principles)

He looked in her direction with a straight face and said, **"it is you that I worship"**, she looked into his eyes and said, **"oh really?"**, he looked back into her eyes and said **"no, not you."**

To worship something is to direct your attention and focus onto something and into something (knowingly by you/unknowingly to you), to the transparent aspect and eternal existence of that thing, not the physical thing/corporeal thing that it is and appears to be, because you see something within it that is beyond it, before it and after it, that is the alpha and omega of its true existence. You begin to see them as just a mortal representation of a quality which is primarily immortal, so they basically become translucent/glass-like to your view and perception, but not to your understanding. To worship is to serve something in pure devotion to its existence (not the physical experience that the existence disguises itself as), and in doing so, annihilate everything about the personated self/personified self and the behaviors of the personality it possesses that may come in conflict with that process and action, within that sacred path to the nucleus of the source of self. To worship is to take a sacred vow and oath within self and onto self, to not veer off thee intended path no matter what distractions may try to interfere along the unknown journey toward the

destination of the known self. The self that knows it 'Is".

    a. Things that control you and influence you and your mind, are things that eventually rule you and rule over you, in another way of understanding, it's energies you unknowingly worship.

        ELABORATION – Whether you know it or not, things that make you gravitate towards its demand, rule over you, and have pretty much full control of you, both mentally and physically (control over how you think and control over how you act), so just in case you don't know/aren't sure what you may/may not be worshipping (unbeknownst to you), just realize what it is that you serve and cater to (knowingly and/unknowingly), when in actuality you should be having that thing serve you and cater to you and your agenda. And if you find yourself worshipping something you don't

necessarily choose to worship, then that means your possessed by that energy and that extreme **"So how do I come out of that possession?"**, the only thing/exorcist who can pull you out of that possession is your own awareness of it, along with your knowledge, wisdom and understanding of it, and an action taken to create space from it **"What is the action I need to do?"** the awareness and acknowledgment of the possession, along with a knowledge of it and being wise to it and its doings will automatically advise you a clear and specific action that needs to be taken to come out of its possessive hold. Whatever it displays itself as, you just be (and thus become) the opposite of its nature and function. Become the opposite body-state and mindset.

b. A thought turned into a feeling/a feeling turned into a thought command an action to be taken/manifested (particularly, a trained-thought and a trained-feeling, from repetitious attention to it). The chemistry of 'action' starts as a biological effect, then turns into a physical/kinetic action (kineticism/movement) **"What do you mean by this last statement?"** what the mind holds in place and within its attention, creates the heart to beat a certain way, thus creating a beat-wave-ripple effect throughout the natural vibration of the inner body, from this the body then matches that template of the new heartbeat and creates a certain chemistry within the biology, mimicking the new beat-wave-ripple pattern while that specific mindset is present. That new chemistry and biology now influences the way the mind thinks soon as the mind becomes absent to the present moment and repeats this cycle over and over again with every opportunity it has to do so. This repetitious pattern/cycle eventually creates itself within the subconscious behavior of the being until the being becomes aware and conscious again to override that program. **ELABORATION** – Every thought seeks to become an action, just like every idea seeks to manifest into an invention. That which is not physical eventually seeks to become physical. You're just a thing in the middle, a circuit, a conduit, a gateway, a bridge/bridging of some sort, a connection of one dimension to another dimension.

c. Which emotions and thought forms have the strongest hold on you? "**Why**?" ... because those are your best friends/closest company and most influential and reoccurring company in your mind and throughout your mind-body, whether you know it or not. They are your gods of worship, your guidance and or guiding's whether you know it or not, whether you choose it or not, whether you accept it or not. Dispelling those specific emotions and thought forms (with your awareness, knowledge, control, discipline and action to do so), is the decoding, readjustment and reorganization of your chosen perception (in parallel with the words and language you choose to use to define and describe your reality and your truth of your experience), which is a perception in favor to your own personal way of living and chosen worship (if chose to), to return the self back to its true-self, the pure untouched and untapped self, the source of the self at its primary level of potential.

ELABORATION – Be aware of what levels of the body and what locations within the body that you become enslaved to, serve to, and start to follow, "**Why**?"... cause that means that that specific section of the body is being overly-active and over-stimulated, possibly by contact, touch and sensation, and it's now communicating back to you with manipulation-like tactics due to the memory you programmed it as (according to its training and programming by you, the programmer), then it begins to feed itself and bring itself to a certain kind of life/life-form by making you subliminally feed it and its function within you, to sustain itself and its existence for its own purpose, despite your purpose.

d. Whatever emotions and thoughts that control the way you think and act, are the very things you work for and work under "**What do you mean by this statement**?" You are under the unconscious command and demand of its programmed purpose, therefore you are possessed by it "**Possessed by what exactly?**" a program. Which in another way of understanding you are consciously-possessed by an unconscious thing.

ELABORATION – Repetitious emotions and thought forms that are on constant replay in your mind (by your non-stop attention to it and focus on it) sooner or later perfect itself by creating a cycle or cyclic way of thinking, and from these internal workings it radiates to the external surface of you which becomes identified by you and others as a "personality", with behavior modifications, and once the mind becomes trapped inside of the brains way of workings (including making its way inside of your biology, blood, nerves, body-systems etc) you become 'possessed' by this energy "**How?**" by it cycling itself internally within you, then orbiting externally around you. The more it cycles, the more it becomes internalized, the more it becomes internalized/insidious the more it goes further beyond the radar of your consciousness and awareness of it, thus eventually leaving you the present being absent of its presence and unconscious of an unconscious programming on constant replay.

e. You can worship something willingly/unwillingly.

ELABORATION – You can consciously/unconsciously create your own 'pull'/'pulling', by giving your voluntary attention to something, or, you can 'become-pulled' into something blindly/involuntary/by chance (due to an unfolding of situations and circumstances you consciously and/unconsciously create and find yourself unraveling within) "**How does this happen?**" by your lack of knowledge of self, control, self-discipline, and absence of awareness. The forces of this reality need your present attention in order for it to become a life-form within you, and need your absence of consciousness in order to live itself throughout you.

f. To worship is to serve. You become a servant (the interesting thing about this scenario is that in actuality you are the master of your own existence, and the body and mind are actually your slaves and or servants. So my question is, what happens when the master becomes a slave and or servant to the slave and servant itself?). The more you unknowingly worship and serve an energy, the more stronger, uncontrollable and influential the energy becomes, soon becoming a continuous expansion of energy (something that was in

your view at first, becomes your area, circumference/surroundings, ultimately)
"Why does the energy move in that way?" because energy is nothing but an extreme/extremity, it has no boundary/limit to its beingness, it just Is, and always Will Be. So in other words be aware and mindful of what energy/energies you are creating and giving attention to cause sooner or later that energy becomes a sphere and orbit around you, having an effect on your mind and perception of life.

g. What we know as worship, goes on within a temple. The body is a temple, and the body contains 'emotions', 'thoughts' and 'feelings', the three things which undoubtedly are your immediate-you (they're connected to your thinking and perceiving, and how you think and perceive is directly connected to your principle of manifestation and or manifesting. Manifesting first within yourself, then secondly, around yourself).

ELABORATION – Everything outside is just a hologram of what the inside is projecting outward **"How is this so?"** through the divine laws of correspondence. It uses the medium of you (the bridge/bridging-thing that you truly are) to interact with the outside atmosphere in order to wake up/activate the inner biosphere, to shake up the biology and psychology in a certain way so that it makes its way to the surface of you and your awareness, **"Why?"**..so that you can 'neutralize' it, **"In the example of a conflicting relationship, triggering me emotionally, how do I go about neutralizing**

that?", by acknowledging the potential trigger with silence, patience, knowledge, awareness, sanity, control and discipline, in order to convert it and transform it into another dimensional formula of itself, and from that, through the principle of an immediate action taken within a mutual space of being. Non-judgmental.

h. Find out the source of your worship/why you are worshipping those specific energies. Question them, question your worship. What's the outcome of your worship? Is it of benefit to you and for you? How do you feel and think after worshipping those energies? (anger, fear, greed, lust, selfishness and jealousy, or bliss, centeredness, silence, attentiveness and patience). How is your mental and physical health after worshipping those specific energies? Does it bring about clarity and sanity?/confusion and insanity? Does it work for you?/against you? Does it further your personal agenda in enhancing yourself?/ does it stagnate your personal agenda in enhancing yourself?

ELABORATION – Every source unto itself (with you being that source) eventually has to seek its resource in order to recourse (if desired to/required to, according to one's need, want or desire to do so in a situation and unfolding circumstance) "**Meaning what exactly?**" meaning if you truly seek and want the understanding of a story and how the character came to be, then you have to first go back to the first page and chapter of its beginnings in the book. In order to rewrite you have to reignite with a new seeing light. In order to return you have to reburn. Burn up the old character in order to bring light to a new one, by first finding out where that character/energy protruded from to begin with.

i. You worship things consciously and or unconsciously (habitually/consciously)
   ELABORATION - In other words, we're beings that direct our attention with reason. But, even though we have pupils to willingly give our attention and focus to a specific focal point, we also possess peripheral vision, which is another form and understanding of attention, an unconscious attention to things around us "**Meaning what exactly?**" meaning you possess two forms of attention, conscious attention and acknowledgment (the pupil), and unconscious awareness and acknowledgment (the iris and cornea).

j. To worship is a certain form of tunnel-vision, solely and intensely focusing on the point of attention, while ignoring the peripheral-reality, in other words focusing on the centered-point and catering to the centered-point, while ignoring/not acknowledging the outer circle which surrounds the centered point/centered dot of attention.

k. When it comes to your mate/partner, if you find difficulty being in unison with their personality, practice worshipping their texture and allure. Don't worry about it feeding their ego, that has nothing to do with you personally, your just privately and silently enjoying your own personal experience within your own touch and/touching, whatever they get from it/perceive from it, and do with it, is their own business, not yours, and has absolutely nothing to do with you at all. Do not feed in, whether they appreciate you for it/not is their choice. Do not expect anything back for your actions and or services, continue appreciating and embracing your experience within yourself, while in company of them/they being in company of you.

ELABORATION – Whatever physically-interactive experience your having, keep in mind that it is 'You' who are choosing the actions being done and it is 'You' feeling those specific feelings, not them "**So how do I balance out that understanding within myself at the moment of interaction?**" Simply by acknowledging and respecting that divine boundary of existence which is an obviously undeniable thing within your experience and experiences. Once you already gain the knowledge of a thing, step aside out of that space of the experience and let awareness, silence and stillness take over that space and become you. Just feel for them, without focusing on how they make you feel. Learn how to internally activate and become activated, without any external stimuli.

1. Worship has absolutely nothing to do with 'expecting in return'/'being-rewarded' (in this path of understanding there's no such thing as "after"/"upcoming"/"sequel"/"arriving" and "expected-effect") "**Why can't I expect anything in return?**" because your being completely genuine with your own actions, by

remaining completely honest with yourself (your heart), and your feelings. Action is a 'Forwarding' thing, remaining a 'Forward' thing only, with no thoughts of an existing behind-thing, because the nature of the word "behind" does not exist in its nature and existence. These are the keys you use to liberate, unlock, and free yourself from the limited psychological boundaries you subconsciously and unconsciously bound yourself to (worship 'principle' for self-devotion).

ELABORATION – This path is based on 'Self-Annihilation', which is obliteration of the ego and personality, to eliminate that which is impermanent at will, in order to come in contact with the aspect of yourself/the self which is permanent "**What's the permanent thing that I am?**" There's no title location or identity to its nature. The only way it can be explained and understood is whenever something leaves, remain aware and present and pay attention to the only thing which remains. Be aware and present to the source of where things occur from, rather than the occurrence, occurring, reoccurrence and concurrent. Seek the platform of a thing, rather than the structure and structuring of its expression.

m. If you choose to worship, worship for the purpose of emotional and mental 'clearance' (to reboot and reset). To 'zero out the register', in order to clearly register the divine channels of communication being broadcasted to you and through you.

n. Texture and allure are principles to worship in another, on another, and within another, and worshipping these principles 'separates' you completely from the person they are/appear to be, and the personality they project. You have an option to practice worshipping sections of an individual in order to then put those sections together in your favor. Worship what the 'feel' is like, just the feel/feeling by itself (mentally separate them from their body/shell) **"Meaning what?"** worship their presence from an energy point of view, worship their essence (separate their personality from 'principality'). In truth, in relation to this path and understanding, their 'presence' ultimately is not about their image/look in totality. According to this specific explanation and understanding, its more about just 'the very proof of their existence' in the very presence of your presence and your existence. It's about the simple appreciation of a simultaneous 2-way acquaintance taking place/middled-point-of-meeting/crossing-of-paths, which in-turn is an obvious 'verification' and 'validation' of some unknown interaction in potential interacting, experience, and understanding, by utilizing the principles of acknowledgment and attention, by simply acknowledging something in your view, and being attentive to that which is in your view (In doing so, keeping in mind and heart that true attention is life/to-give-life-to, so be aware of the attention you give). **ELABORATION** – Since they are you anyway, then giving them attention (their energy, their existence and principle/principles they stand for), is actually giving yourself attention, so in other words an outward directing of attention is equivalent to an inward redirecting of attention on self. 'Your'-self. It's ultimately a win-win situation. Everything here is for you, nothing here is against you, once you know how to innocently and unintentionally manipulate and orchestrate the energies within you and around you that basically 'are' you, then all things remain in a constant return to that which it protruded from. You. The creator and projector.

o. Acknowledging principles and interacting 'as' a principle/as principles with the divine law of principality, keeps you in a mutual harmony of silence within yourself **"Describe that mutual harmony of silence that forms inside me once I acknowledge principle?"** It's a kind of a zero-state of just being, with a deep awareness, patience, and consideration for all things in existence, around you, away from you, that which you have already experienced, anticipate to experience, may experience, and /may never experience. You remain within a limbo-like state of potential and possibility. A state of pure potency. Being neither here nor there.

p. Understand that you were born with slaves/servants/things that already worship you and serve you **"What are these things?"** These things are your 'body' and your 'mind', so that automatically puts you in a 'masters' position of power (you're a master whether you know it/not, whether you accept that reality and truth/not). You have things already set-up in this life/reality ready to serve you, your mission, your agenda, and your intent immediately. Question, when you (the master of your reality and truth) become a slave and/servant to the 'first' slave and or servant (the body and mind), then ultimately, the first slave and or servant (the body and mind) become the 'master', and you (the 'true' master) become the slave and servant to the first slave and servant. When this happens, then the principle of 'leading' becomes dormant, because there is no leader anymore, just a follower following a follower. The leader becomes absent, because the leader (you) is now following the follower (the follower being the body and mind). The master is now worshipping the worshipper.

q. Worship what your focused on. Worship what you have in mind to accomplish. Worship the principle/principles, not the person. Worship the things you are composed of and the things you can compose and orchestrate. But most importantly, worship the principle of action, cause without action nothing will manifest.

r. The more you worship the principles, the more the law and order of principle 'follow' you from one partner to the next, from one projection to the next projection, from one creation to the next creation, from one experience to the next. While the person may disappear, the principles 'remain the same' (the person is not really with you. The person is not really there. The person/persona/personality never truly existed. The principles are the only things that ever truly existed the whole time during the whole experience).

WORSHIP (K.I.M.A.H)

- Keep giving your heart away (keep giving, keep caring, keep loving etc), so that it remains in the outer obit of you and never ever found by the core of you, and remains lost forever in the outer fields of existence. Free yourself completely. Empty yourself completely. Become totally untouchable, totally undetectable, keep doing that until even you yourself can no longer find your heart and love and can no longer possess it anymore. It's not really for you to "possess", it's for you to 'Project' towards and onto. When you no longer feel the need to monitor, manage, and supervise your love-giving/giving of love/love-sharing, that's when you truly begin to become untouchable. When you start to do the total opposite of what the discriminate and judgmental mind says to do (the part of the mind/brain which is trapped in identity), you've become free. Free within yourself, and free as yourself, which in other words is free as 'The Self'.
- Sometimes giving can be ego-affiliated, because giving is set with an 'intent', so don't give, just 'deliver'/let it 'deliver' itself, and just remain a station of 'deliverance'. The more of a fool you feel as you're giving yourself away, is the very

evidence of how much of an attachment you've unconsciously created with your false identity, personality, and ego. In fact, you actually want to feel that fool in order to detect and identify the strength of the glue you've created (over time and experience) with your false self/identity.

STATUES (Principles)

a. Statues don't talk back, communicate/conversate, they just 'Display.'
ELABORATION – You don't always need something/someone to listen to your thoughts and mental dialogue, you don't always need something/someone to vent out on and to listen to you and your personal nonsense **"Why?"** because you don't always need a response, reaction, input, advice and opinion from an outside party cause the more they react/respond to your output, the more it will create static, and the more static that's created the more difficult it is for clarity to be realized and utilized for balance of self, and from that, the more the potential and possibility for self-reflection is neglected and abandoned in your reality. The ego lives for feedback, the spirit remains humble (in silence and stillness) and can care less, because it does not expect anything in return, cause according to its reality it's the only thing that exist, the only thing in existence, so who/what would it be talking to and communicating with? Or expecting from?

b. Statues are stilled-representations of live-functioning platformed-principles, in still-mode
ELABORATION – It's helpful to recognize realize and know principles exist, but it's also helpful to possibly see them/their physical-representations as well (if possible) **" What physical representations?"** In other words,

an on-going, a 'being'-thing and existing thing which reveals its subliminal existence and purpose in human animation, but in a state of pause, such as the pose/poses of a human-bodied statue.

c. Statues are things that just are. You need just-are things to acknowledge, to give attention to and to focus on, without any returned-static and any returned feedback (just like principles). **ELABORATION** – You need things around you (that don't possess a mind and personality) to stare at, focus on, concentrate on, and zoom in on without the thing noticing you committing that act towards them **"Why so?"** so that you can become lost within the thing/things completely with no distractive feedback, in order to dive into a state of nothing, without feeling the need to explain yourself and your actions to that specific thing/anyone. Learn to give to a give a thing/project to a thing which doesn't necessarily receive, but just displays.

d. Statues are just things that display and don't play/take action. By something not playing back/in-action with you, you get to have a clear and private space to self-reflect within the orbit of your you-ness **"And what do I get in return?"** which in-turn promotes enhancement of your uniqueness/uniquity (You-are You-nique).
ELABORATION – A viewing/displaying alone of some-thing can inspire, which in other words trigger the activation of your most innate potential.

e. A statue is a status **"And how does status relate to this understanding?"** Status is a standing, an understanding like a standing statue, which in other words subliminally represents principles you stand for and principles that stand for you.

f. Statues are impersonal. Humans are personal. If you want to come more in contact with that which is impersonal, with your impersonal nature, you have to acknowledge (and interact) with inanimate objects and impersonal representations/impersonal symbols and symbolisms.
   ELABORATION – "that which interacts with that is that". You reflect that which you come in contact with, and connect with (the divine laws of correspondence) **"Meaning what?"** In order to be that, you have to see that.

g. Statues are still-posing symbols/symbology's that remain in your view and endlessly speak to you and through you in silence and presence **"How so?"** through their stances and poses, symbols and objects, atmosphere and environment, body and face expressions.

h. Statue is a status (def: status – a standing of someone/something).

i. Interacting with something in complete silence (with silence in return), lets the mind open up and expand in its vast emptiness of pure potential and unlimited possibility within the realm of self-reflection, without any outer-interference and mental distraction **"And what happens from this?"** and from this, clarity, sanity and centeredness arrives in one's moment and beingness. From this, the principles of patience and consideration begin to develop and mature. And when one returns to the present moment, they handle human situations from a more humble and impersonal state of existence.

j. Act as if your partner is a statue you're worshipping. Worship the outstanding qualities and principles you appreciate about them, worship their presentation and their display silently within self, all the way down to body parts and specific detail and eliminate their behavior and personality out of the picture (since you know the personality isn't real anyway).

k. Find out the principles they represent and find those same aspects within the posing and the expressions in a statue, and create/purchase a statue that represents those principles of them for this specific reason and your specific doing. And when you go back to communicating and interacting with the person and their personality, you'll respect them more as a person/"individual", simply by perceiving them through the truth of principle. Create an alter for the principles they possess, not the person that's possessed.

l. Finding the principles within an individual makes you look at them more like a god/god-like figure, and respect them as a god/god-like figure **"And what does this mean?"** which means you respect the space and orbit they exist within, and you let that god-like force navigate itself in whatever direction and path it chooses, whether it navigates itself from its own ignorance/wisdom, towards its own progression or degression, and towards its own constructive/destructive state of mind and design **"And what comes about from this**?" From this point of understanding and perceiving, you undoubtedly know that you cannot and would not want to steer another life in any way you personally and selfishly would want it to be, you know for a fact that a life/living being evidently and ultimately steers and navigates itself throughout its own experience by its own divine birthright. Now you know you have no choice but to let go and let be.

STATUES (K.I.M.A.H)

- Acknowledge your partner and be attentive to your partner through your peripheral vision, rather than facing your partner face to face in frontal-view (gradually eliminate their person from your reality).

- Instead of looking at your partner talk, just hear and listen to them (like only a voice is present, not the person. This helps/assists you in not becoming so personal with your partner).

- Stop looking at them at every move they make, when they're facing you walking towards you and have their back to you walking away from you/your area.

- Practice having and holding a straight face (while still going through whatever feelings, emotions, and thoughts that may arise, while not ignoring and denying whatever may arise internally, psychologically, and biologically).

- Practice not reacting, only responding if you feel/know the need to.

- Never spill your ill-emotions and ill-thoughts onto your partner, deal with them silently in stillness within yourself before responding (if you feel to respond within that very moment/later after the moment has passed).

- Be willing to confess your wrongs/wrong-doings/imbalances you contribute and have contributed to the situation, first within yourself, then with your partner, if you feel the need to do so/choose to.

- Practice kissing your partner with your eyes closed/eyes looking elsewhere

- Embrace parts and sections of your partner, like the lips, neck, skin texture etc (rather than the person/personality). Practicing this begins to separate you from the friction and personality.

- Embrace the possibility and response of the word 'no'.

- Never revenge/do in-spite-of

- Learn the principles of patience, stillness, and silence

- Get out of the hopeless-romantic mind state

- Be open to the understanding and principles of graduation and possible transformation within process and progress of a relationship/partnership (the 1st grade is not the same as 3rd grade and so on and so on).

-       B e flexible and willing to adjust and adapt and survive any terrain, circumstance and situation that promotes and supports self-enhancement and self-growth internally (/mentally).

-       Get interested in yourself as much as you have interest in your mate (what talents and gifts do you naturally have? enhance and invest in that).

-       Practice acknowledging your partner without emotion (doing this practice doesn't mean to ignore any feeling/feelings silently and privately within you, just feel it without making an external expression of it, because feelings are a certain indication/certain indications, an informing of a possible realization of some sort).

-       Embrace your partner as principles (the specific principles they display), if the personality and behavior is not in-sync with who and what you are (principles like care, nature, attention, communication, contact, interaction, hospitality etc.. instead of trying to accept their dysfunctional repelling personality, embrace and worship the principles they animate and are composed of).

-       Space and opportunity are synonymous to each other in the understanding of sustaining/sanity/reclaiming sanity in one's mind. With space comes an opportunity for self-liberation, self-involvement, and realization of self-relevance/recognition of self-value.

EMBRACE DISLIKE (PRINCIPLES)

He said "**Wow, this space, gap, silence and distance that we created or was created between us made me realize things within myself that I wouldn't have seen and realized without it**", she replied "**what have you seen or realized within it and throughout it?**", he replied "**pure revelation and realization. That which wouldn't have been witnessed and accepted without it. Thank you**".

Embracing "dislike" is equivalent to acknowledging the gap and space which is always in existence between two things whether you were aware of its existence before/not. When I say "dislike", it's not really meant to be looked at as a "disliking", it's just about being aware of two mirroring-principles which have always existed, and these two principles being 'Attraction' and 'Repellant'. That which brings 'Together', and that which remains 'Apart'. The word dislike itself is more of a judgmental disguise of a bare principle which has nothing to do with judgment whatsoever. The word dislike comes from a more side-picking judgmental point of view, which activates the identity, animates the personality, and triggers the emotional body/soma-body (according to ancient knowledge and wisdom). Keeping one trapped inside of an egotistical-cyclic-reality between the actions of thought and behavior.

a. Dislike equates to 'Space' and 'Distance', and space and distance (when acknowledged and recognized by one) brings about one's privacy and self-reflection **"In what way?"** It brings about a self-reunion. It makes you remember you, the self, remembering itself.
ELABORATION – When you dislike someone/someone's 'orbit', you keep away and stay away from that being's orbit as much as possible to prevent a certain friction and/conflict from happening, and that orbital space/orbital-spacing matures into physical distance, and that physical distance develops into mental space and mental distance. You are now in private commune with yourself, your thoughts, your inner-noise and inner-silence, and your private mental dialogue, a dialogue which has no one else and nothing else to communicate with, and once that's realized by thee awareness of the being, that dialogue becomes more and more silent, that silence creates more of a gap between the being and its mind activity, and once that space between the being and its mental noise is recognized, the volume of the mental noise begins to lower and eventually disappear and the being is once again by itself, and to itself, enjoying the reunion of itself back to itself, leaving the being and its emptying silent mind no choice but to reflect back upon itself because there's nothing else present but the being and its silence within its own aloneness and stillness.

b. The action of 'self-involvement' and 'self-interest' is the automatic effect and/end result of a dislike for another/other **"Due to what**

exactly?" due to a confrontation/intense argument held between two mates, that ultimately separated them from that heated moment and parted them in different directions of each other for an undetermined period of time.

ELABORATION – Being life ourselves, we naturally involve ourselves in life's situations, and create friction/face friction in life's situations, and the outcome of that specific imbalanced situation, in-turn, become open to potential and receive things automatically as a reciprocal effect into our life because of that imbalanced situation that occurred. That's a natural thing that happens in this life, due to the inevitable principles of void and fulfillment. We sometimes do that/share that/play with that quality willingly in verbal relationships and or physical relationships with people, and even if we choose not to play with that quality of inclusion anymore with someone, that quality/automatic function in life will naturally happen, which means that if no one is there for you to do that with, then it automatically does it with itself and within itself immediately, as self-reflection.

c. Dislike is also equivalent to a 'repellant'/'repelling', the opposite of attraction. Repel and attract, attract and repel, are nothing but ying and yang, respective qualities, respective polarities. Learn to respect principle itself **"What does respecting principle mean?"** respecting principle has nothing to do with your emotions, thoughts, opinions, and advice on it and of it, it just is as it is, as it always was, and as it always will be. Just remain aware, acknowledge, respect, and accept/align with what things that just are, as they truly are, and reveal itself to be.

ELABORATION – You don't necessarily have to consciously choose to dislike someone, you'll just naturally realize that something just isn't getting along/flowing your energy and another's energy, something just isn't flowing and existing in a naturally-undisturbed-harmonic-balanced-rhythm, and both of you just aren't able to come together like two magnets of opposite poles facing each other. The energy just naturally repels each other, regardless of one's logic, like, need, desire, and want for another, or one's need, want, and desire for things to be.

d. Dislike is just as important and relevant as closure **"How so?... explain please"** true space is closure, and true closure is space. No matter how tight you close your fist, you can still fit a toothpick, safety pin, or needlepoint in between that small space between the palm of your hand and the closest finger against that palm. Once this obvious truth is realized, with common sense, it's considered and respected in any way and every way of understanding in life. Enjoy and appreciate the space and distance from each other. One polarity polarizes the other and brings about the projection of the other.

ELABORATION – Being alone brings about self-reflection. Self-reflection brings about closure and acceptance of what is and all that is, and in-turn, that closure flowers into openness of self, and openness to all things in existence. Your only able to come close together because space existed prior to the action of coming close together.

e. Dislike doesn't mean hate/despise.

ELABORATION – There's no logical need to hate principles **"Why?"** cause without the existence of principles you wouldn't be. Principle isn't a personality/person with a specific intent towards you because it possesses no brain for distinction and agenda. Principle is the foundation of what is known as personal. So, hating/despising/disliking principles is equivalent to a life hating/a life showing resistance to its own life and existence, it just doesn't make any sense at all according to common sense. Principles don't have a mind/a personality, you do. Only that with a mind and personality can do something with an agenda/intent behind it, so if it doesn't possess these functions then why have emotions towards it? When these emotions arise, the only thing that needs to come from you is awareness, stillness, silence, and understanding (that alone matures into a wisdom and knowing of what is, and what self is).

f. Embracing dislike/a repellant/a space, is respecting and enhancing the principles of expression, creativity, ability, capability, the principles of draw-back/return, retreat, the understanding of source, space, truth, revelation, magnetism, the witnessing and understanding of attraction, individualism, self and self-reflection, reflection, receptivity, interception, patience, orbit/orbiting, privacy etc **"How so?"** simple, it encourages self-reflection, and out of self-reflection comes about unlimited potential and possibilities of self.

ELABORATION – With the understanding of what is, comes the respectful-acceptance of all that reveals. Embrace, accept, and neutralize the principle of external-revelation within thee internal-self.

g. If you have an issue with the principles of dislike/space it means that you're addicted to bondage/glue/gluing/desire/desiring/possession/pleasure. In other words, within your ignorance/unknowing, all you really seek in another is territory and property, not freedom and respect **"How would you know?"** because according to the laws of polarity (which is a divine law everything in this existence is governed within), if you're not moving out you're staying in, if you're not going down your rising up, if you're not being pushed your being pulled. To make a long story short, seek liberation and space.

ELABORATION – To dislike is to create space from another and/others, so if you don't like that space and/accept that space and gap (which appeared on its own), then that means you're stuck in the opposite direction of that, which is to bond to something, to remain stuck to something, a something which is being pulled apart from you by unknown forces from occurring situations and circumstances that unfolded **"So what should I do?"** simply acknowledge what is, and align with what is without judgment. Period.

h. Dislike occurs in order for you to recognize the glue and to play with the glue, for you to determine how far the glue can stretch before it snaps/comes back together.
ELABORATION – When you dislike something/someone, you seem to be coming and going, you come back to one/back to a certain center/centering, and then once again go away from someone/away from the center and vice-versa, so it's like an energy which is versatile and flexible, an energy which has the ability to stretch/extend, to leave and return, return and leave whenever feeling the need to do so. If that energy was physicalized it would be similar to a kind of glue/a rubber band.

i. Dislike also assists in a respectful release (with a knowledge of what is respect and a knowledge of what is release), in the case/possibility of a transition/one who has transitioned (it also works/is also useful in the situation of a break-up, split, or divorce) **"How so?"** because the occurrence of dislike/repel brings about an acknowledgment of one's space and a sense of respect of one's space, and one's nature, and in-turn a respectful and open-minded knowledge of self, as an effect (and reflection/reflecting) of the one your becoming spaced with. A respectful acknowledgment of an occurring gap that is creating itself, and having a knowledge of what a gap/space is, you gracefully let it be, because you understand that space creates closure, closure within yourself, and possible closure/cohesion of the relationship you're in.

ELABORATION - The more someone gives you a reason/reasons to dislike them/not like them/to not be around them, the more the gap and/space matures into an acceptance of what is, and that acceptance of what is matures into an unexpected-release (a letting-go and letting-be), no matter the situation/unfolding of events that may occur. That releasing soon matures into a respect of what is and what is to be and become.

j. Don't become glued to neither like nor dislike **"Ok, so what should I do then?"** just be aware that your composed of a device which naturally discriminates/differentiates this from that, what may be beneficial and what may not be beneficial, what works for that moment and experience, and what doesn't work for that moment and experience, what supports an agenda, plan, goal and idea, and what doesn't support it. That's it. Like and dislike cannot be an identity/your identity, only if you take it personal and get identified by these devices then you become possessed by them, lost within them, and begin to identify yourself as them. A building is not defined by its elevators and escalators, the elevator and escalator are just things to get from one level to another, that's it, the building remains the same regardless of its internal functions and operations, because it's only a function and operation of the building, inside of the building, not the overall identification of the building.

ELABORATION – You have a left-brain hemisphere and a right-brain hemisphere, you are composed of two opposing-complimentary-existences **"Besides what I'm composed of, where does the I exist within this understanding?"** you exist somewhere in between, and you exist as both things as a whole, so in other words it's irrelevant to pick a side, because picking a side is like favoring only 50% of your existence and embracing only ½ of your experience. Each side only exist to support itself, don't get caught inside of the siding-game.

k. Both like and dislike are things which you unconsciously attach to (and may identify with). Never deny/ignore what's evident/what's unfolding from a natural interaction of communication between you and another connection of some sort.
    ELABORATION – Like and dislike exist in the brain, so ultimately, it's all mind-play/brain-play to be exact (while keeping in mind that the brain is the place where identity exists, so be aware to not become identified with these mental-functions, to not define your being by these discriminating functions of the brain and mind).

l. To feel a sense of dislike/to recognize a repellant/to realize a repelling presence is good awareness-exercise. Look forward to losing yourself within the moment, in order to learn how to find yourself within that same moment (before that moment passes). This exercise/practice shows you who and what you really are, and are really about, besides who and what you thought you really were. This is a self-revelation method and technique.

ELABORATION – Awareness/to be aware, is to accept if and when you slip, and to remain aware of how far you may slide at the moment of slipping. With sharp awareness, you slide a very short distance, with a dull awareness you slide a very far distance **"Which means what?"** which means you may be going in circles, going in cycles, and potentially going insane.

m. The very action of you being pushed away is the very evidence of something unfathomable pulling you towards itself "Explain" Push and pull are one of the same kind, one polarity cannot and does not exist without the other. What's pushing you and pulling you has absolutely nothing to do with your mind, your intent, your thoughts, and your ideas, because it is something which occurs out of nowhere and steers you out of your own control, apart from your logic and rational thinking. Looking in the face of one is staring into the face of the other. Co-existence (they exist amongst each other, because of each other, for the existence of each other).

ELABORATION – This is a split-reality, where both sides of the orbital-split are simultaneously constantly pulling you into its own individual orbit, into its gravitational pull, but according to your perception and understanding of life you call it a push and pull action, when it's really the principles of repellant and attraction, electricity, and magnetism. The science of inevitable unification.

n. The hatred and/dislike you feel within and identify over time will become a physical thing inside your body. Locate it immediately. It's usually a section where biological contraction and constriction occurs, which are the internal sections/locations of energy stagnation (which are internal identifications of hatred/dislike), located in the anal canal, rectum, lungs, heart, etc. The outer signs of identifying/identification you can visibly identify are the tightening of fists, gritting of teeth, the flexing of muscle, the appearance of vein on muscle, the squeezing of the heart (creating a heart attack) etc **"What do these visible identifications represent?"** these are sections, spots, and locations where hatred, dislike, aggravation, frustration, and agitation reside within the body. Basically, where emotional pain houses itself within, places where it gets stored, blocked up, blocked in, stagnated, and stuck within. Once this happens you may find yourself in reoccurring-cycles of a routine and situation, which as a result, keeps this stagnated energy in place between time and space.

ELABORATION – The reason your mate can make you sick (if you're not aware and don't have any control/discipline of self), is because you've unconsciously made them one of your organs inside of your body. This is a natural phenomenal occurrence when two individual beings willingly keep another within their orbit and experience. Over time and time spent, a merging and/infusing happens. Both experiences enter each other mentally and physically to create the divine-androgenous agenda, and since both genders have both genders within their self (both estrogen and testosterone) the phenomenal divine androgynal elixir is inevitable (depictions of ancient gods and goddesses give reference to this androgenic truth, with both gods and goddesses possessing characteristics, facial features, body-types, and phenotypes of both male and female qualities). That which isn't physical seeks to be physical. The life force that you truly are is the crossover from one existence to the other existence, through you the crossing is held, you cross things over knowingly and unknowingly, you manifest the potential/unmanifested, into the possibility. The evidence/traces inside of your body of this crossover that's taking place, expresses itself in the transformation of your organs and health. Free-flowing energy, stuck energy, and trapped energy, that in itself expresses itself as the display of your personality, behavior, and character on the outside/external.

o. Embracing dislike is estranging your partner from yourself, and that estrangement creates the presence of a stranger (a known but unknown stranger, the stranger being your partner), and once both of you become strangers to each other in that moment, then potential between you and your partner arise once again to possibly become a new possibility, a potential to create and begin a brand new and fresh love connection, if chosen/agreed to do so. Every time this strange phenomenon of estrangement occurs, a potential, possibility, and opportunity for a reboot, reset, and clean slate becomes possible, only if it is recognized and realized with pure awareness, compassion, and consideration from both partners/parties, that's the only way the whole can move as one again. Without that it cannot.

p. As much as you like, you must equally dislike. As much as you dislike, you must equally like. Sooner/later you'll realize that they're both different forms of navigation and direction, not things to take personally/to personally identify with. Certain things in your life (according to who and what you are in that moment in your life) are of benefit to your growth and enhancement of who and what you're developing into. The reason I chose to touch upon the understanding of dislike is because people think it's a bad/negative thing to feel and/experience, and it's not, it's just an experience, and nothing more.

q. To dislike/recognize a repellant/to recognize a naturally-repelling-presence is good 'Awareness Exercise'. Look forward to 'losing yourself' within the moment, in order to once again 'find yourself' within that same moment (before that moment passes). This shows you 'who' and 'what' you really are and are about, besides what you thought you were and are. This is a self-'revelation' method and technique.

EMBRACE DISLIKE (K.I.M.A.H.)

- The dislike/repellant energy you may be detecting from the other (non-discriminant and non-judgmental energy), take that as an opportunity to turn inward and ignore the outer-interaction and outer-interference and make that a desolate thing, abandon that within the space it's signifying to be within and leave it there by itself, and sooner/later the energy will neutralize itself in mutuality.

- The dislike thing is not a negative thing (it may be implying the principle of space).

- Regarding dislike – In the event and case of a venomous and/poisonous bite, or in the event of an argument, dispute/confrontation, to prevent poison and toxicity from traveling and circulating throughout the body and brain, it's best to respond, rather than to react.

{SIMILAR PROCESSES IN 2 DIFFERENT SITUATIONS TO BRING ABOUT THE SAME RESULT}–

A bite – Relax, don't look at the bite, the strike/wound, breath slow.

An argument – Don't pay attention to the opposing thoughts circulating in your mind, just witness them, remain patient, listen, be silent, and respond without judgment and emotion when clear to do so.

- Let that which speaks for itself speak for itself

Sound derives from silence, so silence is equally important as sound, utilize both moderately. Every solution doesn't need to be spoken. When utilizing silence, utilize action.

- Let them come and go as they please

Just as you appreciate the arrival, appreciate the departure as well. Out of sight out of mind, thought and imagination. They have legs, will power, prerogative, ability, choice and decision, and there are doors and windows, an outside and inside to this reality. Keeping this simple mind structure keeps one who is in respective acknowledgment of these obvious advantages and opportunities humble within their self, and in acceptance of all things possible to be and potentially become.

- Appreciate space

Voids become filled on its own. Get into yourself with every moment and opportunity that arises, that's an example of something you are, speaking to you. Find out what it's saying and do what it's saying.

- Your mate acknowledges you and gives you attention

Let the principle of attention be itself by itself and do what it does without your mental input. It's a kind of direction and directing, there's no need to direct it/redirect it, it doesn't need you in order for it to be. It appeared, and will be, regardless.

COMMUNICATION AND EXPRESSION
(Principles)

He said " **I'm in expression right now, and my expression within itself is communicating to you, and through you in this very moment, are you open to it? do you see it? do you realize it? do you feel it?**", she replied " **I already know how you think, what your gonna say, and how you act**", he replied " **so show me your crystal ball. Once you begin to think for me, predict for me and predict about me, and act for me, then what other faculties do you leave me as my own to operate and function as in the presence of you??**"

    a. If your mate feels they must second-guess and/think-twice before they talk to you, touch you, and penetrate you (based on your repelling-response and repeated behavior towards them), it'll eventually create more silent unconscious unwanted and undesired hatred and dislike for you, unbeknownst to them, and unbeknownst to you as well **"How does this begin to happen?"** Thoughts will start to roam around in their mind, thoughts that will become 'enemy' to you. They'll begin to shell-up and close you out from their reality silently and subtly, knowingly, and unknowingly, voluntarily and involuntary, for the protection of their own feelings, emotions, and sanity. To their perception, you'll turn into nothing realer than a dream/imagination that they can only see, witness, and visualize, but can never grasp and interact intimately and sensually with, so in other words (according to the abandoned one's perception) your real living life will inevitably and ultimately turn into something 'fake' and 'no longer real' in their reality. You'll begin to seem like an intangible thing to them, and sooner/later their 'focus and attention' will direct and or redirect itself elsewhere where it is acknowledged and considered, whether they personally desire it to be that way or not. That's a form of sexual and sensual torture (a form of mental torture and biological torture), a form of 'involuntary-celibacy'. Celibacy should be by choice, not by no-choice or force. Acknowledge freedom, realize freedom for what it's worth, and let freedom rain and reign. Live and be, give and be free with your loved one/beloved. Never force them into repression, holding back their full expression to you, putting them into a psychological and biological self submission of some sort. Sexual nature and sexual urge are things that you cannot logic with and rationalize with, and if you think "you can", then understand that it can only be "tamed" but for so long. And keep in mind, that the longer you hold it off, the 'stronger' it gets, and the stronger it gets the more uncomfortable and possibly uncontrollable it becomes within you.

b. A penis or vagina is not an "extra-accessory" which can be moved, replaced, or taken off, it's a natural extension of your natural body, on your natural body, connected to both mind and body, through a hallway of nerves, within the grand hall of electro-magnetic energy.

c. Talk, touch, and penetration or insertion are the main 3 ways of 'communication' and 'expression' within an intimate relationship or partnership between 2 individuals sharing an experience together, and all forms of communication and experience need to be 'free' to communicate and express at any time it feels necessary to, and both must be receiving and returning of these freedoms in order to get the true message/messaging given and left by the other messenger. Don't discriminate against the delivery.

d. **Talk** – body language (poses, stances, and animation), speech to ear, fingers to the body, toes to the body.

e. **Touch** – hand to hand, hand to bare body, body to body, lips to lips, lips to body or body parts, tongue to body or body parts, skin to skin or contact to contact.

f. **Penetration** – penis inserted into vagina, vagina on penis, finger into vagina, hand on penis, tongue into mouth, tongue into vagina or around vagina, tongue into ear or around ear.

g. Love is like a play or playing of existence, when the play or playing is cut off, the fun starves, the interest is no longer there, and the attention redirects itself elsewhere 'on its own', regardless of where and who the individual would like it to be on or rather it be at (regardless of one's feelings, devotion, commitment and care for another, and agreement with another, that "another" will eventually become replaced by 'an Other'). Your carnal and intimate desires sooner or later overpower that. Desire doesn't know what the word "wait" means, those words are not within its vibrational vocabulary. That falls on the minds responsibility to set a pace for the body's 'needs and wants.

h. 2 ways of 'communication-interaction', hearing and listening (verbal), and observing and responding (physical, or feeling and response).

i. What we call communication is 'free-flowing-oscillation'. When both sides are oscillating then both sides enter into further dimensions of existence together. When one side stops or stagnates an oscillating force then the force dies in that direction and redirects itself elsewhere, toward another side willing to receive and remain receptive to its oscillating-forwarding force **"Give me an example"** an example of this scenario, is kids that don't have fun playing with mad, sad, miserable, or depressed kids. Kids like playing with other playful kids who are happy and joyful and imaginative just like them. When a happy and joyful kid starts playing with a kid who is expressing/projecting a low energy, the happy joyful kid finds someone else to play with somewhere else almost immediately.

j. We use 'arms' to reach and make contact (which is a form of forward oscillating-communication). We utilize 'speech' to reach and make contact. The 'beating' of the heart beats 'outward' to reach. Exhaling is a kind of reaching to make contact with something. Seeing, looking, and viewing is a certain kind of reach or reaching and making of a contact (like making eye contact with another), that which is local seeks to become distant', until that which is distant becomes local, all within reach of its proximity. To make contact with that which is close, near, distant, far, further and furthest.

ELABORATION – You are here to make contact, interact, transact, transmit, transmute, transform, transit, and transcend.

k. Communicating with plants and trees (within an orbit of self-centeredness and balance) gives the plant-life a kind of life and liveliness to its nature and its beingness. It seeks your attention and communication so that it may express itself in different ways and different forms within its atmosphere.

COMMUNICATION AND EXPRESSION (K.I.M.A.H.)

-       Whenever situations you unfold negatively/off-centered, and you want to remain true to your heart and hearts path and feel a need/want to talk touch and/penetrate your partner, you must proceed with the desire and intention in the very moment you feel it, and if the response you get from that is repelling then remain exactly where you are/back off, back away and disappear from that space back into yourself, and if it happens/occurs more often than not, then reach out to them no more for an undetermined period of time, and recede back into the core of your orbit, ignoring the existence of them. That unintentional counteracting action you find yourself doing (which is ignoring them or remaining in your own orbit and space), is obviously what they're promoting to you (known/unbeknownst to them) that they request you respect.

-       Be completely true and honest with your feelings and emotions for your mate and act on them immediately (while ignoring/not feeding in to your opposing thoughts), and hug them, kiss them, embrace them in some way in the midst or dissipation, of an argument, dispute, disagreement/potential confrontation. When in friction, confusion, anxiety, stress, aggravation and agitation within mind body and moment, take an action, because to take action is to keep yourself present and out of the frequency of cyclic thought. Worship the principle of action and take immediate action (within that very moment) of your genuine feelings and emotions for your partner towards your partner, while being completely true and pure with your hearts-intention and nothing else. Witness the thought and/thoughts and the forms that thought take and transform into, see or witness the view of thoughts, acknowledge the view and distance between you and that view, a space appears, discover the space of suspension from your thoughts and eject from the seat of your thoughts, before that plane of existence flies into a high mountain top and explodes on impact (the impact being the collision of emotion and feeling within the body, created from the minds attention to it).

-       Dislike is also realization but utilize the realization that you receive without judgment and emotion towards your partner, and just purely embrace the unrequested receiving gift of realization itself.

-       Dislike is also retreat, it is the 'you' being given an opportunity to return back to yourself/itself, to retrieve the treasures of clarity, awareness and sanity you left behind, that you need to activate and take back out with you into your present reality.

-       Communication is the gluing of the spirit back to itself, and in-turn, the disappearing of both people/communicators, as the result and evidence of its reunion. By worshipping the principles that another possesses, it brings more of a mutual and neutral flow of respect, communication and interaction with them and their personality (it makes interacting with their personality a lot less stressful and you become more tolerating/accepting of their personality, in other words at the very least you'll be able to accept,/endure and bare with their personality a lot better and more free-flowing, keeping the communication and interaction staticfree).

-       If verbal communication isn't making the connection, then experiment with distant-body-language, if distant-body-language isn't making the connection then experiment with touch/physical contact, and if touch/physical contact isn't making the connection then experiment with space, silence and self-involvement (magnetic and attracting qualities. A draw-in). find the correct method of communication in any and every given situation. You must always be willing to remain humble no matter what, in order to figure out the formula which Is best for that specific interaction in that moment, space, and time.

TREAT OR TRICK (Principles)

A patient man once said "**I have to treat you and/this accordingly, otherwise I trick myself**"

"**What do you mean by this statement?**"

It's not necessarily and ultimately about treating an individual a certain way, it's more about being aware, patient, and remaining receptive to how a situation is unfolding and revealing its ways to you on its own, and in-turn of this revelation, you begin treating a situation a certain way, while still at the same time remaining true and genuine to your heart, your path, your doings, and your own private experience within you "**How do I do this? ..** by navigating yourself through a path which you realize is actually creating itself. The other individual (the individual which is displaying the friction, or the challenge, for better words and understanding), automatically and simultaneously receives the tailed-end and aftermath of that specific treatment and treated experience (being treated a certain way by you), and may realize that tailed-end revelation in return as a potential lesson/opportunity for their own self-reflection, if chosen by them to commit that action and do so. The individual on the receiving end (the individual receiving the friction/challenge) will begin to automatically manipulate and orchestrate energies and forces knowingly and/unknowingly, in reflection to the situations and events unfolding before them, while being in conjunction with the others low-vibrational-activity and reactivity, I.e. constant anger, frustration and confusion (which is being consciously and unconsciously projected onto the receiving individual repetitiously).

ELABORATION – Every action has a reaction, unbeknownst to us, our agenda, and our intent. Every cause has an effect, unbeknownst to us, our agenda, and our intent. Everything is governed under the divine law of principle, and polarization, whether we're aware of it or not, whether we're knowledgeable of it or not. Under every folding is an unfolding, and vice versa. From that constant unfolding and folding of situations and events that two individuals start and or find their selves within, both parties receive the end result of those folding's simultaneously, which in turn, impacts the experience in a certain way. Similar to the nature of a ripple effect, the rock dropping in the middle of the pond is symbolic as the conflict/friction created between two people, and the ripple effect created from the impact of the rock making contact with the pond rippling outward, is end result which both people receive.

Low to no self-control and discipline over a reactive personality, being easily subjected to personality and identity possession, leaves little to no possibility for a gap/space to appear in one's mind, for the potential of a clear moment to arise with pure self-awareness (awareness being the screening and filtering of the madness, to filter out the madness before a state of mind goes mad).

When it comes to deciding the treating of a situation, as its playing itself out to be, from the view of a patient and aware individual (within an imbalanced relationship), the treatment, and ways of how it should be treated silently and privately inform the patient, aware, and receptive individual how, when, and where to respond, and when and where to take action, what to respond to, and what to become active with. From this private revelation and realization within them, they begin to move accordingly, and exist accordingly, in order to maintain their own balance and centeredness of both mind and body.

LIVE/LOVE (Principles)

He said " **Hi... I'm Here!... I'm Alive!** ", she replied "
**Yes I know... I see you!... Yes I know your
alive!..**", he replied " **No, not "alive"!... A – LIVE!...
A – LIVE – Thing!... HERE and NOW!** "

According to this specific path and
understanding, the words 'love' and 'live' are
synonymous to each other/somewhat related to
each other, first, through the similar spelling of
both words, and second, through the subliminal
understanding of both definitions, through the
filtered understanding of metaphysics primarily,
not just from a dictionary. To be live and
acknowledge your own liveliness is to be of the
moment and of presence, to embrace the moment
as it is and as it reveals itself to be in that
moment, space, and time. To love/be love/be in a
space and orbit of love is to embrace what has
made its way to the surface of you, through you,
from within you in that moment. It is ultimately
something that exists and resides privately
within you. To be love is to be live, to be live is
to be love. Being live and being attentive to
another's liveliness/livelihood, is keeping
another live within their self, and keeping
another live to their self and within their self is
equivalent to keeping another zoomed in on the
focus of the love within their self that they
radiate, and emanate that expression of that
specific radiation outward, with you and towards

you on the receiving end as their chosen main focus of attention.

a. The best thing one can do for another they care about is keep them live, which is to acknowledge them, to keep them within the divine moment they exist in, to give them your attention. What good is 'love' without attention/being attentive to your loved one? (you develop love/care for someone because of how they're projecting their self/animating their self to you/towards you/around you, which is based on their 'principles'/principles at play) **"What is attention?"** Attention is 'life'. Life is all. That is why a baby which is a new life, screams, yells, and cries for your 'attention', because it is pure life, an untouched and untampered form of life, a life which seeks your acknowledgment and attention to acknowledge and give attention to its own life to keep itself live. The reason why every living thing has an 'image' and 'presence' is to be 'noticed', interacted with, and 'acknowledged'. It's the very reason why nature is so full of beautiful bright colors, vibrant colors, everything seeks your 'acknowledgment' and 'attention' towards its existence and experience, to validate its existence and experience.
ELABORATION – What is the point of having life around you if you don't acknowledge the life which is living around you? It is the very reason why people talk and sing to their plants in their home, and when

they talk and sing to their plants the plants grow in beauty and abundance and blossom **"Why do plants grow when you're singing to them and/around them?"** simple, vibration (which is sound) equals manifestation (which is geometry/geometrizing/growth/development, expansion and abundance). People also talk to their pets, and when pets are acknowledged and talked to and interacted with, the pets become full of life and aliveness and want to interact back with you and play with you, keeping their life youthful, healthy, and happy. To acknowledge is to validate. To attend is to sustain.

b. It is not 'love' that someone misses in a troubled relationship, it is 'attention'. Attention is 'life', and what we call life is something which is 'live'. One prefers their 'liveliness' to be acknowledged, and to be given some level of attention to their existence. **ELABORATION –** What good is a location without a direction/a directing. What is the use of having a dartboard without having a dart to throw at it? In other words, what good is a view that isn't being viewed? How pleasing can it be? And in turn, how pleasurable can it become to itself and within itself?

c. Would you want someone you care about to say "yes I love you"/"you know I love you", and never acknowledge you/give you any attention?.. or.. would you rather someone you care about to acknowledge you and give you attention without the verbal-confirmation of saying they "love" you? Which is the silent confirmation and validation of that truth. Acknowledgment and attention is a certain kind of language-like thing that leads to verbal-communication, verbal-interaction, body language and physical-interaction. **ELABORATION** – Acknowledgment and attention is the gateway to unlimited potential of that which is, into that which can be.

KNOWING AND FEELING (Principles)

She looked at him with tears in her eyes and said " **I care so much about you! How can you not feel it**??".. he looked back at her with a straight face and replied " **I don't know what you feel, I can only feel what you know** "

    a. No one knows what anyone is feeling/thinking, one can only feel and/somewhat sense/detect what another is about.

    b. Nobody can be in any other body but its own. No mind can be inside of any other mind but its own.

    c. "I don't know what you feel" – A feeling/feelings are sacred and private only to the one experiencing that specific feeling. Even when one is describing/explaining their feeling/feelings to you, they themselves may not even be describing it that well/that precise to a 't' **"Why not?"** because they're in feeling mode, and feeling mode can sometimes lack intelligence, logic, and rational thinking in that specific moment, so once again, how would you be able to know what they're really and truly feeling? And how strong that feeling might actually be? If even they themselves might not even be actually aligned mentally and energy-wise with their own experience in that present moment.

"I can only feel what you know" – one (/the receiver/the one who is on the receiving end) can only feel and/sense something from another/the other, and that feeling and sense is received as unidentified and hidden, so in other words the receiver would have no way of specifying/pin-pointing what it is exactly that they themselves are feeling and/sensing from the other, they can only feel something, something indescribable and unexplainable (but exact in its own way), because feelings are blank states of existence delivered with an intent and intensity of some undetermined volume. It just says "I'm present. And you know that I'm present". "I occur with no label, title/description, just pure me. You figure it out". "You know for sure I'm definite and absolute, whatever else you're unsure about you figure it out". Never count on anybody else outside of your body, to 'know exactly' what your 'personally' and 'privately' feeling within your body and your energy (that just doesn't make any sense at all). Never put that responsibility and/weight on any-body and any mind, that wouldn't be fair in any way to the person/the union you share with them.

d. Every-body is busy/occupied creating their own body and feelings and feeling-body/body of feelings throughout their experience. Don't interrupt that experience and that growth development, that experience and development is for them to own, not for you to interrupt/disrupt in any way.

I OF YOU (Principles)

She looked into the eyes of her lover and said, "**I love you**", he looked back into her eyes and said, "**I love**".

{**Def**: **OF** : Expressing the relationship between a part and a whole. Expressing the relationship between a scale/measure and a value.}

An alternative way of saying that statement (and understanding that statement) is "I of you", implying that "I am of you", and in return, "you are of me". Individually we are first completion (by ourselves, as ourselves), together we become ultimate completion (dive companionship), meaning, individually we are both part and whole, but together we are a part which is a whole, and a whole is a part.

In stating this truth from the path of the heart (which is the true self true to itself only), leaves mental room for self-freedom and self-liberation, the freedom to escape/eject from physical bondage (within an emotionally charged experience and bondage) at moments/glimpses of need/want. At will. In other words, always possessing the key to the lock when needed/wanted to be utilized, according to the situation at hand, for the sustainment of mental and emotional balance.

"Why did he reply like that? What does that reply mean?"

In the example of this dialogue, she, has directed, addressed, and localized her inherited free unlimited energy-force. He, on the other hand, chose to keep his inherited free unlimited energy-force in its own natural freedom, without a focus to target it towards and bind it by. The one who is receiving the statement and response of "**I love**", if their awareness is absent (with only their identity and judgment present), will see this seemingly indirect statement/response as offensive, careless, heartless, insultingly indirect, and somewhat confusing.

When looking at the statement "**I of you**", as far as the word 'Of' is concerned (meaning representing a part and a whole, or minute and abundance), it's a word that almost seems like it's presenting something/about to present something that hasn't yet been presented, so the perception of the word itself remains somewhere in the in-between worlds of existence, neither here nor there, a nowhere from an unknown somewhere in a way, so basically by pronouncing this word with this statement and using this word and statement to represent you, you just 'Are', and the word 'are' is subliminally describing the anonymous-totality of the 'All' (You) that the nothing (You) truly is, so in other words by saying the word 'Of', connected within the statement, and truly meaning it, you basically remain undetectable, untraceable, and untouchable by all things and thing, including yourself and your own logic. Equivalent to 'full-release' at will, 'true-departure' from your personality-creation.

    a. "I of you" is the same thing as saying, "I am of you". Meaning "I am made of you" and "you are made of me", that, in itself, is in a way subliminally implying parts, and together validate the whole **"How so? In what way?"** a whole individually (as their self, by their self), and a whole, collectively (by their self, but amongst another self). 2 separate complete-parts/total-parts (within their own individual respective orbit of totality) sharing a cohesive orbit of one experience, creating the whole experience.

ELABORATION – Everything is 'whole' by itself, and as itself (being that each individual has both traces of estrogen and testosterone within their biology, both masculine and feminine), but as far as 'pairing'/'companionship' with another, is another understanding of the word 'whole', which is known/more related to the word known as 'wholeness'. The understanding is we are both gods/projections of a god, so in other words she sees this thing called god as a 'man', and he sees this thing called god as a 'woman', and in that middled-seeing is the unified understanding of the 'whole' as 'one'.

b. Saying "I of you" leaves more of a lighter feeling within you, but still deeply validates (and makes the point) your in-depth and most innate connection expressed to your partner, confirming a tight connection from your heart to your partner, validating a sacred bond, which is bound.

ELABORATION – It validates a freedom-like bondage/bonding-like freedom. Relatively foreign in a way. Be aware of what words and vocabulary you choose to use/utilize to describe your reality, in other words be aware of the words your mouth is saying because your ears are listening, and your mind is interpreting what's being spoken.

c. "I of you" is an 'obvious', yet 'cryptic message' all in one. Seen and known but hidden and unknown, but not doubted nor questioned. The statement validates itself in another world/existence/hidden perspective.

ELABORATION – Remaining in the middle pillar of existence gives an equal amount of freedom of choice in which polarity you choose to have your experience within, while maintaining your sanity and mental-clarity for balance of self.

d. It sounds right, feels right, unharmful, and respectful. Makes the mind puzzle, figure, reorganize, and perceive, reassuring an unknown-known, and felt thing. Strangely comforting, non-threatening to the feelings, may make you use your mind and question the statement, and in doing so, leaving room for an open discussion and conversation, with the listening, willingness, and potential to expand your mind and alter your perception. Yet endearing, a unique and rare bondage and freedom, secure but flexible, sharing one space together, while at the same time remaining within your own private individual space. A representation of void and fulfillment, satisfaction.

ELABORATION – Never fight the feeling, deny the feeling, or question the feeling, let the feeling do what it does to you, within you and through you, without any following judgment behind it.

e. "Of you too" is a statement which validates a kind of eternal-connection of some sort. It also validates the aspect of mirror-imaging, reflection, a reflection which is self-communicating with itself, through the medium of another voice and experience. It vanishes you and vanishes the other. Validates a personal and impersonal confirmation. Letting me be me and you be you. Respecting you individually by yourself. Letting you stay where you stay while playing where you play. Letting yourself be yourself and letting yourself be thee itself, thee itself which it is and can only be. It's like receiving something and receiving nothing at the same time. It's as if it is you who is speaking to yourself. It's actually an example of spirit coming back in contact with itself, through the adhesive-medium of a thing called language/self-confirmation and self-validation, through the medium of an instrument called sound, projecting itself as a 'voice'.

I OF YOU (K.I.M.A.H)

- Practice silently validating your part in their life, rather than speaking, saying and stating to them your part and role in their life. Let them figure it out and see it/realize it on their own, without your help/assistance/input.

-       Stop speaking that which is obvious (if you feel a need/want to speak for that which is obvious, then you never let what is obvious speak for itself and express itself naturally).

-       Practice not pronouncing your feeling and/feelings, begin to act on your feeling and emotion immediately, especially at the moment/moments you don't want to act on them. Just keep in mind that your only being true to your heart, feelings and emotions for that specific individual (minus the negative thoughts/opposing thoughts that pop up about that specific individual in the very moment of the feeling and emotion seeking loving and genuine action).

LOVE AND LIKE (Principles)

She said "**What? What do you want? I love you!...isn't that enough?? What more could one possibly want?!..**", he said "**I rather you like me**".

a. Using the example of a boat on a sea, when in comparing this example in relation to a love established relationship between two individuals, what we call 'like' is the free unpredictable movement of water in the sea, and what we know as 'love' is the boat that moves across the face/surface of the moving water on the seas. Without water/moving water, a boat cannot move. Love is a thing which becomes activated/comes to surface at one point between two individuals who hold a special connection, that validates itself in a specific moment and time. Like is a present on-going thing, which has the potential to keep that past moment and time anew and present, keeping an open door with unlimited access to infinite possibilities.
ELABORATION – The boat is stability, a stabled thing (stillness/a stilled-thing), the sea is mobility, a constant moving thing (movement). In another example of love and like when in relation to a love established relationship, but using the examples of 'ground' and 'gravity', 'like' is the gravity, and 'love' is the common-ground that remains held together by the gravity, so without the present force of gravity the ground falls apart. So without the existence of 'like', the experience of "love" begins to fade and split in separate

directions experience-wise. From one shared experience, into separate experiences.

b. On-going relationships/relationships that remain in continuation from equal-interest in one another, go from 'like to love', to 'liking to loving', then back to like and like-ing (the 'ing' at the end of a word implies going, growing, flowing, forwarding etc, to keep the already-past-confirmed energy present and still-valid).
ELABORATION – A shared agreement/a created-focus (agreed, created, and focused-on by and between two people, with two points of focus focusing on 1 point together) develop and go through a maturing process as the joint-experience continues in harmony between time and space.

c. To like is to keep a bind, to love is to create a bond. To like is to keep a bondage presently bound, to love is to create/keep a bond/to reminisce on a past bond, without a need for a present reunion/present binding.

d. Love can somewhat survive without touch/contact, like seeks to touch, and likes to remain in immediate contact.
ELABORATION – Love is maturity, like is playfulness. The 2 formulas of life/being. We grow and develop in this experience through levels of parallelism, from one to the other then back to the one – from play to maturity, from mature to play, and so on and so on back and forth. Like turns to love, but love needs like in order to keep itself going in a specific direction (physical contact and verbal interaction).

e. Love is longevity, like is eternity.

ELABORATION – What good is a "long time" without the existence of 'eternity'? What good is reception without service? Time is imprisonment and quantity, eternity is freedom and quality. Time is a set-price, eternity is true-value and pricelessness.

f. Love is the settling/the settled, like is the interesting, the interested, and interest.

ELABORATION – To be settled is to be stable/stabilized, but if interest remains present during the stable experience, it keeps the stable experience in a state of 'Flexibility'/a flexible existence.

g. Love is the opening of a door, like is keeping the door open.

h. Love is the burn out/burned-out, like is the burning.

i. Like and love can co-exist simultaneously. Sometimes love can exist without like. Like seeks to transform into a kind of love/loving/love-for/love-like thing, within your radar/under your radar.

ELABORATION – Like can subliminally transform a certain texture of love into a different texture of love/different textures of love, turning the once-was texture of love into different textures and fabrics of itself.

j. Love is something which happens individually within you which you can take with you by yourself, like is a thing which happens from you (extending forward and onto) which keeps you in company of another/the other, and vice versa when the love and like is received in harmony by the one was projecting it first/keeps it in projection.

ELABORATION – Love is an inward-pointing-arrow. Like is an outward-pointing-arrowing.

k. Love is private, like is public.
   ELABORATION – Love is an 'impression' (a self-impressing impression), and like is an 'expression' of the self-impression.

l. Love validates that a like/liking has taken place at one time in the past/passing/may still be present (this is evident when you see that what we know as 'like' slowly/gradually seeks itself to graduate into a love, which is the next grade of itself).

m. Like is adolescence maintaining a maturity, love is maturity with potential to play as adolescence

n. Like is possibility, love is potential
   ELABORATION – In the beginning of an acquaintance maturing into a relationship, like is potential and love is the possibility. Then as the relationship matures and both individuals are pretty much used to each other and used to being around each other (after disagreements and events of friction), like becomes a possibility (a possible reoccurrence) extended from the potential/lifeline of the love-foundation.

o. Like keeps the life present in love (without like, love may disappear and be nothing/no more)

p. The best thing you can do for a loved one/someone you deeply care for, is to live them (pronounced LY-ve, as in the phrase "live on the air").. not love them (what you call love is a private thing, a thing based on you within yourself, not something within you that you can share with someone else)

ELABORATION – To keep someone live/to acknowledge someone's liveliness/live-presence is to acknowledge. Acknowledge is to direct-attention, directing attention turns into interaction and interaction matures into physical contact. By doing this you're showing that you like them.

q. The 2 main things people look/seek for is love and god, and that's why they can't find neither one of them because it's inside of them (inside is a place and space where most individuals never search).

r. Attention and acknowledgment are way more powerful than love, and the only way for attention and acknowledgment to be is if like is in play and present (therefore like is more important and more valuable than love, because you must like someone to a certain degree in order for you to feel the need and want to constantly acknowledge them and their presence and give them attention, as a reflection of them holding your attention primarily).

ELABORATION – What we know as like, is a thing which becomes activated/and may remain active, which remains directed towards a specific target/its specific focus, and devoted to that specific target/focus which activated it and its potential to be.

s. Like is based on interest, and interest is a certain kind of direction/directing-towards. You can set the direction/directing in 2 different directions simultaneously – 1, within yourself, by genuinely liking yourself/your own company, your mind, which is increased interest in self, and like for another, and vice versa simultaneously as well. And 2, interest for another and interest in another, and like for yourself. Both directions can grow and develop at the same time, simultaneously, and parallel to each other.

t. Once like is gone in an on-going relationship/connection, the mind and emotional body go through certain schisms, because the mind and feelings created a specific memory-base for that specific experience, and when that experience is no longer functioning and operating according to what the memory bank is familiar with, it will first begin to swirl in psychotic cycles and then emotional cycles, and those cycles will ultimately expand if the awareness is not present/doesn't remain present. Like is a bridging/the bridging. Love present between 2 individuals are equivalent to 2 islands separated by water without a bridge. Without like (or enjoy) the 2 islands (of love) will never become bridged-together.

LOVE AND LIKE (K.I.M.A.H)

- Find out where you're at in between both worlds. Feel out both spaces of existence and fill out both spaces of existence, to identify which is what/the differentiation and distinction of one from the other. Observe the unfolding of events and situations (with awareness) with each principle individually before you group them up together and move forward as one movement moving forward in your experience.

-        "Being in love"/in a love doesn't necessarily mean that it's with somebody, it just means that you yourself are inside of the space of love, and you're feeling what being in the 'space of love' feels like (the person and personality your person is and the other person and personality it's physically interacting with, is just an impetus/incentive).

LOVE SONGS (Principles)

a. Most so called "love songs" have addictive and obsessive lyrics within it, emotionally-charged expressions, implying an obvious need and/want by the artist that's present creating the specific rhyme rhythm and reason **"Hmmm.. interesting. Explain. Such as... ?"** such as lyrics like "I need you, I want you, you need to be with me, not him/her, I can treat you right/better than them, I'm better for you, come stay with me, he/she isn't good/right for you, if you don't be with me I'll kill myself, I can't live/breath without you, I can buy you this and that, take you here and there, you need me, I need you, I was made for you, you were made for me, we were made for each other, we belong together, we're going to die together, we should die together, I'm not taking no for an answer, you don't know what's best for you, I know what's best/better for you, they're bad and I'm good, I can treat you better/good/great, leave him/her for me, let's be together, you know you want me, I can make you happy/happier, you belong with me, I belong with you, we belong together, come inside my car/house, look how much money I got, I can buy you this &/that & he/she can't, I can take you here and there, come with me, trust me, have faith in me &/us, we were meant to be, please be with me talk to me and look at me, drink with me and smoke with me, think of me, touch me, ask about me, go out to eat with me, leave him/her now, call me, text me, embrace me, recognize me!".. ETC!!... these are all selfish-commands and demands, that look sensitive, soft, innocent, "endearing" and nice, with rhyme and rhythm behind it as its 'Disguise'.

ELABORATION – A murderer rapist or serial killer looks like a nice, pleasant person, with a pleasant gesture and a smile on their face (but hidden intent). Every being is composed of a disguise of some sort, just as the spirit disguises itself with the uniform/costume and mask of a human being. Remain aware of the representation and that which the representation represents/derives from.

b. They all at some point throughout their songs, repeat these 7 words and statements such as 'I, I am, I'm, Me, My, Myself, Mine' **"So what happens if I repeat these same words while I'm singing?"** .. As you repeat these same words while singing along, their reality (whether real/fake to them and from them) turns into your reality, from what's being sung out loud/expressed mentally. Be aware of what you speak into existence. These 7 words are known as 'Reality-Crossovers'. The phrases:

'**I**' - I love you, I want you, I need you, I can't take it anymore.

'**I am**' - I am the one for you, I am the one you need and want.

'**I'm**' - I'm lonely, I'm sad, I'm mad, I'm in love with you, I'm your man/woman, I'm the one you need and want, I'm good for you, I'm a great lover, I'm a good man/woman.

'**Me**' – You're the one for Me, you need &/want Me, call Me, you and Me forever and ever, you belong with Me, come with Me, follow Me, look at Me, be with Me, Me and you, Me and you should be together.

'**My**' – Be My girl/man, My My My, My baby, My love, love of My life, this is   My girl/man/baby, My way/the highway, you're My girl/man, be in My life/world, come to My place/car

'**Myself**' – I'm by Myself call me, I don't want to be by Myself, how can you leave me by Myself? don't leave me by Myself, I can't be by Myself, I'm just here by Myself thinking about you, I'm here by Myself thinking about you, I'm here by Myself missing you

'**Mine**' – Be Mine, you are Mine, she's Mine, he's Mine, this &/that is Mine, all Mine, you need to be Mine, whatever I want is Mine, this car/house/world/money is Mine, this woman/man is Mine.

: These '7 words' are the 7 words that are the closest to our subconscious minds that we always choose to use and speak into existence when we are representing ourselves or defending ourselves, in a specific identification of ourselves and to others. These words create a reality and truth, and validate a reality and truth, and the very speaking and pronouncing of these words is a 'giving of permission' by 'agreeing' to its terms through the magic of the composing of the terminology being used to bring-that-specific-thing about. When defining and describing ourselves by saying these words first to begin a sentence, phrase, and quote, we're agreeing that these first words spoken is the very introduction to who and what we are in that moment/who we are totally, and the words which follow right after (that follow right behind the first word) represent the definition and description of who and what we really are. The first word is the 'context', the words that follow are the 'contents.

c. The more we consciously repeat these words, the more they echo in our skull and brain **"What happens in the brain during these echoing of words?"** .. the more they echo the more they move into history, then into our memory, then into our subconscious mind (from consciously relating ourselves to the words which we speak in the present moment), through the realms and colorings of feeling and emotion, then into the subconscious mind, and from there you sooner/later begin to think and act unconsciously from a subconsciously programmed base/foundation of being. **ELABORATION –** The more deeper something embeds itself within you through repetition and repetitious behavior, the more you become susceptible to unconsciously acting-out these ways and ways of thinking. The deeper it gets within you, the deeper you get lost within it, knowingly and unknowingly.

LOVE SONGS (K.I.M.A.H)

- Instead of singing these words and thinking of a girlfriend/boyfriend/past mate/past love, act as if you're talking to your heart, soul, spirit, essence/existence itself. Make it more of an immediate intimate relation, rather than something which is distant. Bring 'you' more closer to 'you'. Keep you to 'yourself' completely.
- When singing along with songs, practice saying the words "they, them, him and her", instead of saying "I, me, my" (doing this will subconsciously begin to create space and distance from the singers experience, truth, life, life-story and their perception, and from this you begin to release from their emotional and mental trauma that they're singing about, and will automatically return back to your reality clear-minded, clear-hearted, totally detached from their personal drama and traumatic history.
- Act as if you're singing to your heart/spirit/soul, not to "another'/someone else/something else outside of you/something else distant from you. Practice standing in front of a mirror and looking at the middle of your chest where your heart is at while singing (don't look at your face or into your own eyes) or close your eyes and dedicate the melody to the darkness/unknown aspect of you.
- Stop investing your emotion into songs, which is nothing but a union of words and sound, specifically orchestrated into a certain rhythm, to bring about a specific chemical reaction within the body, and to bring about a certain perception within the mind. In a way of

understanding, it's a form of unintentional manipulation/intentional manipulation. They're all devices and mechanisms for pulling one 'into'...

-        Look at a music video on 'mute', and study it, and see if your still emotionally connected to it. Keep in mind it's the illusional choreography and orchestration of many different things moving together that draws an illusional reaction out of you. Another practice to do is listen to a song you really like that moves your body and keep pausing it and playing it, pause it then play it, pause it then play it, and keep doing this until you identify the very thing which pulled you into it to begin with, and to recognize that's it all just a moment (and possession) that only lasts for about 3-4 minutes of its playing time, and realize the true insignificance of its existence within your experience, by seeing that once it finishes and goes off your right back into the silence of life that was there before it, and will always be there after it.

GLUE (Principles)

She looked at him and said, "**I don't think it's working out between us**", he replied "**I think you're right. So this is where it ends. Thank you for the experience. Goodbye**". As they began to walk away in opposite directions she soon turned back around and asked him "**do you feel that?**"

a. Glue is 'Goo'
   ELABORATION – Every physical thing in existence has a 'Texture'. The texture itself possesses certain qualities to its nature. The qualities itself possess evident principles of its beingness and doingness by itself, and with interaction with other things which come in contact with it. The principles that are witnessed, observed, analyzed, and known, are an obvious fact of its physical existence. The principles reveal its true nature and true purpose in our experience of it, and interaction with it, and as it.

b. Every relationship, companionship, and partnership are based on a 'gluing' of some sort **"Meaning what?"** We create glue without a clue.
   ELABORATION – We meet to join. We join to bond. We bond to bind. We're born in androgyny, to become one androgenous being in unison with another individual/another multitude of self **"Meaning what exactly?"** meaning anyone and everyone that you know, derived from 1 womb and 1 exit. Even if you

were to say that there are many people who exist in this reality, I'll entertain it and say "ok, but even those woman/wombs who gave birth to those "many individuals", "collectively", still derived from 1 womb/1 exit. So, no matter how you look at it (in the understanding of "multitudes"), there would be no "multi" without the existence of single/singular".

c. Attraction is 'magnetism', magnetism is potential 'glue', glue is potential 'bondage', bondage is potential 'unification'.

ELABORATION – Anything that's in the process of a coming-together/a together-coming that is happening out of our control and apart from our intent, is something we exist with, exist within, and exist as, something which we live with, live within, which lives within us, and live as, and something we must understand along with its workings, to understand our functions.

d. Different textures (and stages) of glue and gluing (Elmer's glue, crazy glue, gorilla glue etc)

ELABORATION – There's different energy forms of bondage/bonding, that takes place in a connection between 2 individuals. One starting form can enhance into a stronger cohesion (depending on the connection, time and experience between 2 individuals), and that strong cohesion can transform into a stronger bond/tighter bond and so on and so on. The different physical brands of glue validate the different levels of glue/gluing one may find their self within, within the process of an experience accompanied by another experience, sharing and creating one experience together **"How so?"** every living thing/live thing within its own orbit, naturally draws, attracts, and pulls things into its orbit/cypher. Whether perceived as beautiful/hideous, it automatically draws 'attention'.

e. Be aware of the strength of the cohesion of the glue/glues you create as your creating them (awareness is key, and consciousness is the turning of the key within the lock). Depending on the strength, durability and flexibility of the glue that's been created, determines the difficulty/challenge of breaking free from the bondage between you and another/others (that which you're gluing yourself to, knowingly/unknowingly, voluntarily/involuntarily).

ELABORATION – No matter how strong the glue/gluing becomes over time and experience, as long as you remain aware/have awareness of the gluing factor, the glue/gluing can always be pulled off, peeled off and pulled apart. The glue never gets stronger than the awareness (along with the principles of control and self-discipline). And as long as the principles of awareness and action are hand in hand with each other at will (when desired/needed), any glue and every glue can be separated immediately.

f. Acknowledgment, attention, attendance, participation, volunteering, interaction, time, experience, sharing, caring, affection, commonality, familiarity and action are the creating and building factors of glue, and the trans-texturing of glue (along with contact, feel, touch, kiss, and penetration/intimacy).

ELABORATION – Keep in mind of the glue-making procedure as your creating the glue, and/as the glue is creating/manifesting itself around you, amongst another, and with another.

g. Glue and glow are synonymous to each other metaphysically, that's why healthy sperm glows, and is also a kind of glue with glue-like texture and abilities (like stickiness), and is the same color as things that glow in the dark. Which is why the more you ejaculate in and on a woman, the more you become more attached to her, and vice versa for the woman's vaginal secretion on a man, becoming more connected to him energetically and spiritually. And also is the reason why sperm creates a gluing effect between 2 individuals called a child/baby, which keeps 2 individuals glued in each other's life for an undetermined period of time.

h. Thinking and thought are other kinds of glues as well.

ELABORATION – The mind and body has devices to glue you to itself **"Like what?"** passions, addictions, obsessions, thoughts, cravings, lust, sex, taste, touch etc, to make itself real in your experience, by crossing itself over into your experience, to validate its bodily purpose.

i. Elmer's glue, super glue, crazy glue, gorilla glue, e6000. Which glue are you oozing and creating? (wood glue, adhesive, polyurethane, snail trail, glue stick, epoxy, rubber cement, aleenes, j.b.weld, kwikweld, feibings cement glue etc).

ELABORATION – Remain aware of how attached/attaching you are becoming/have become to another throughout the passing of time throughout your experience, while experiencing it.

j. What are you gluing yourself to? Why do you want to give yourself to that thing? The quality and texture of the glue/adhesive will determine how long you will be stuck to that thing. Be aware of the glue which is oozing from you. Strong-glue-bondage creates a slime-trail in its aftermath, implying a potential continuance of its nature (a slime-trail is evident of a previous strong hold. The evidence of a strong-hold are the remnants of its contents within the slime-trail, and the existence of the slime-trail itself).
ELABORATION – Glue (without one's present awareness), in the example of bonding to another in a relationship, is potential for one to become territorial/looking to own another/the other.

k. Glue is a middle/middled thing. A thing which is created and/placed between 2 things. A thing which bonds and looks to bind. Something which keeps 2 obvious states of existence together within 1 orbit of reality. A thing which appears in the middle of two things which are in contact with each other.

l. Be aware of who and what you glue yourself to throughout your experience, cause that will determine the extra weight you carry/are presently carrying with you, and the extra weight being carried by you determines your speed of how you're moving through life, and the slower your speed the more you become susceptible to time and all its baggage it possesses (in another way of understanding, glue brings about a certain kind of weight/weighing down on one's pace/speed through life, and the more you weigh, the more you sink). Also, being a victim of time is equivalent to being a victim to the past, within a present phenomenon which only exists in the present moment, so in other words, the present vehicle (you), can keep/remain something which is no more/no longer (the past) within its gift and treasure of the moment, and from this-doing, the present being never gets to experience its true present-nature, and will only be able to see and interact with present life from a past point of view and perception. This is an example of presence being glued to its past. The more things that are glued to you, the more you drag and crawl through life, when you could've been walking, sprinting, speed-walking or jogging through it. Metaphorically speaking.

m. Be aware of the memory you create on your body and within your brain (or brain-body, because the body itself is the biggest brain). Memory. along with being uncontrollable, undisciplined, jealous, angry, resentful, regretful, spiteful, hateful, lustful and selfishness (amongst other lower energies/anchoring-energies), determines the subconscious-stronghold and unconscious-influence of the glue your subjected to, knowingly and/unknowingly. The body and brain are nothing but things that experience, gather, accumulate, collect, project, animate and express. With keeping this in mind, you will become more aware of your interactions and actions with things you keep around you and find yourself around.

n. Habit, repetition, and cycle, create a stronger and stronger glue. The more constant these 3 principles keep reoccurring and rotating, the deeper and deeper it becomes embedded within the density of your nerve-network and the blueprint of your perception, thus creating your reality, your truth, and your lifestyle, unbeknownst to you and your intended manifestation of it. As the 3 principles consciously cycle, it goes from your conscious mind (which is the filter/filtering process of the mind, the detection/detecting point of mind, the voluntary part of mind), piercing through that and into the subconscious mind (which is the undetected actionary part of the mind, the part of the mind which is involuntary and remains on replay), then falling deep into the abyss of the unconscious mind (the deepest undetected and anonymous part of the mind, the part of the mind which the conscious and subconscious mind can remain forever lost within, if a spark of awareness never occurs within the individual). In other words, the cycling process is a constant sinking and anchoring process, reaching deeper and deeper depths of the mind which are beyond what a being can fathom.

TYPES OF GLUE/FORMS OF GLUE

Craft glue/witchcraft glue
Wood glue
Super glue
Fabric glue
Hot glue
Passive sensitive adhesive (PSA)
Glitter glue
Epoxy
Polyurethane
Spray glue
Glue pen
Glue dots
Glue stick
Tacky glue
Elmers glue
Mod podge
Crazy glue
Gorilla glue
Rubber cement
E6000
J-B weld
Titebond
Dap weldwood
Ultrabond eco 980
Dap rapidfuse
Loctite
Liquid nails
Flex glue

TYPES, FORMS, and TEXTURES OF GLUE

Acrylonitrile
Cyanoacrylate
Acrylic
Recorcinol glue
Epoxy putty
Ethylene-vinyl acetate
Phenol formaldehyde resin
Polyamide
Polyester
Polyethylene
Polypropelene
Polysulfides
Polyurethane
Polyvinyl acetate, poly alcohol, poly chloride
Polyvinylpyrrolidone
Rubber cement
Silicone
Silyl modified polymers (Def: Polymer: A substance that has a molecular-structure consisting chiefly/entirely of a large number of similar units bonded-together, e.g., many synthetic organic materials used as plastics and resins).

o. **Natural glues/gluing-agents on and within the body** – Saliva, blood and mucus is also a certain type of glue, glue-like thing/gluing thing. Your magnetic-field is also a pulling-to/gluing thing. Therefore, glue is related to the word 'Goo', because glue is not just something you consciously and unconsciously create, it's also something which oozes from you physically, through the textures of saliva, blood and mucus.

p. Communication between 2 people is the gluing of the spirit back to itself, and the slow disappearing of both people. By worshipping the principles that another possesses, it brings more of a mutual and neutral form of respect, from this point, communication and interaction with their personality becomes a lot less stressful and you become more understanding, tolerating/accepting of their personality (you'll be able to endure and bare with their personality a lot better and more free-flowing, keeping the communication and interaction static-free).

GLUE (K.I.M.A.H)

-       Practice feeling and describing the glue/pull/magnetism that's present between you and another.

-       See how long you can stay apart from each other, remain quiet in the house around each other, see how long you can go without communication and interaction until you can no longer go on without acknowledgment of each other.

MAGICIAN (Principles)

a. You make things happen, appear, and occur with your mind, with your need, your want, your desire, and your intent, almost all the time (around you and distant from you), whether you know it/not.
ELABORATION – Need, want, desire and intent are magnetic and element-orchestrating qualities of your mind and the electro-magnetic energy field of your internal body. You draw things up, then draw things to you. "**Why is that? How is that?** "... because of the principles of 'Void' and 'Fulfillment'. Every void seeks to be fulfilled and will be fulfilled, and every fulfillment seeks to fill a void and will fill that void. It's also why actions like 'intercourse' exist, and why there's two polarities of existence in this experience, because one seeks the other consciously, subconsciously, and unconsciously, sexually, mentally, and physically. So, in saying that, the principles of need, want and desire, are the void/voids which are magnetic things, and these magnetic voids become fulfilled. These are things/vacuum-like energies that pull in outside realities, inward towards itself, in order to carry out its specific agenda "**Can you give me an example?** ".. another way of looking at this, a painter only paints a picture (the void) because someone somewhere (unbeknownst to the artist) wants to purchase it, and will purchase it (the fulfillment), a song is only being created (the void) because someone

somewhere (unbeknownst to the musician) wants to hear it, and will hear it (the fulfillment). Just like every thought (void) seeks to become an action (fulfillment), and every idea (void) seeks to become an invention (fulfillment). It's about a hidden-crossover/crossing-over from one side to the other, and you just exist somewhere unknown in the middle of these two realities and polarities of existence. Through you, they come, and will be.

b. The past and the future can only be born from the present moment, cause what you know as past and future can only be brought about into existence through the present moment, the present mind, and present being (you). **"Which means what exactly? ".**. Which means that neither past nor future exist, and it is merely a 2-sided projection of the 1 projector in the middle. In other words, presence itself is both the mommy and daddy of past and future. This is something to understand. People, situations, places and events that appear and occur in your experience become a 'part' of (and are 'connected' to) your past present and future realms of existence. **What do you mean by that?..** for example, lets say you seen someone an hour ago at the store, then you seen someone else by the mailbox in your building 25 minutes ago, and then you seen someone else in your laundry room 10 minutes ago, these different people and places now exist within the catalogue of your memory, and at any given time you can choose to go back in time to any one of these places in your mind and recall the whole situation as it was, while being in the present state. Your mind and heart is the creator, manipulator, and orchestrator of all 5 elements (fire, air, water, earth, and 'Time') and all 3 dimensions of existence (then, here, and after). The true and real time machine is you. You infuse time-sequences, and travel to separate sequences of time at any given moment when requested/desired to.

c. The time-vehicle (your body and brain) is directly connected to the time environment (your immediate surroundings, area, and atmosphere) **"So what am I? ..** You (the essence) are the median conduit between 2 placements of correspondence, which possess the unlimited potential of infinite interaction, that becomes live at any moment the minds intent directs it to be

   ELABORATION – You are the connection, connector, bridge and bridging between the gap of 2 oblivions, polarities, orbits, and existences. Without I, there is no "It".

d. Whatever you really, truly, genuinely, and honestly want and/feel the need to be, that force itself remains devoted at your feet awaiting your true demand and command to manifest itself solely for the purpose of your specific agenda being held within that very moment in mind and heart **"Why does that happen? ..** because you are electro magnetic static, a static magnet, meaning whatever you magnetize within, and zoom in on, releases itself outward as an electrolyzed static, pulling in that magnetization back to its magnetic source from which it derived from/protruded from, to complete its full circling form once again. And from this point, the cycle then repeats itself over and over again, spouting out and pulling in, pulling in and spouting out. **ELABORATION** – All is you, and for you, and you are all, and for it.

e. Anyone and everyone that appears in the presence of your acquaintance, appeared as a need/want/desire that you have sieged within the abyss of your subconscious and unconscious voids, so in other words, principles appear as a person with a personality, to interact with the personal aspect of your personality, to connect with the principle of you, in order to make contact back with itself as the true principle that it is and always was regardless of the disguise it appeared as in front of you "So is my primary state of being just principle and principality? .. Yes. It's all you, coming to you, to interact and connect with you, from this intersection of interaction you have the power to manipulate the unseen forces and orchestrate unmanifested events in your favor. **ELABORATION** - everyone appears in your life as a thing which fulfills some kind of void/voids within you, whether it's communication, interaction/sexual/all 3, you are here to fulfill your voids for a sense of completion/completeness/total, to form the illusional goal/ideal-goal of wholeness, within this bodied form.

f. You are a thing which draws things up from a 1-dimensional plane of mind and envision, into a 3ʳᵈ dimensional drawing, into the end result drawing, a drawing which appears as a person and/setting, and then draws that thing/those things to itself immediately (and or simultaneously) **"Give me an example please"** .. This process is in relation to the same development as an atom into a molecule, and that molecule into a compound, a grouping, clustering, accumulating, and gathering process. You pull and orbit things into your cypher. Since you are composed of atomic-action, you unconsciously behave like an atom and orbit things around you and your nucleus (atom-molecule-compound) **ELABORATION** – The macrocosmic is an expression of the microcosmic. You mimic, act, animate, and express yourself externally in the same exact way of how your biology and energy functions and operates internally, and those external/outer expressions are seen and known as personalities, characters, and behaviors.

g. Magic just means to make things happen out of a nowhere, and to make things appear out of nowhere **"How often does that happen? "**.. You do that almost every day/every time you really need and want things to appear and happen for you, for a specific reason and purpose, to bring about a certain result which supports and sustains your agenda to be. **ELABORATION** – When it comes to life, isn't that the same way you were born?.. you appeared out of nowhere, but you still appeared somewhere. Here.

h. Anything coming out of a dark hole/dark tunnel is magic, anything that appears out of a nowhere location into a somewhere location, anything that transforms into something which it wasn't before is a form of magic. Anything that just occurs/happens in the mental direction of your intent is magic. Calming down an intense situation is magic/magical.

i. The brain sitting inside of the skull is equivalent to light/mind/thoughts thinking inside of a dark cave, this is why you can manifest things into 3rd-magnitude from 1st cursory **"How so?"** .. because anything that is a dark container/carbonated containment conceals the conduction and production of potential energy transference, and once a light is sparked within that darkness (with an intent as its navigating force), it bounces throughout that containment and banks off itself consistently until it finds a release of its force through an opening of some sort which appears, but through that chaos that its going through inside of the darkness it gets stronger and more powerful.
    ELABORATION – From a screen/flat plane of existence which is thought/thinking mode, into a pop-up plane of existence, and from there into a physical/tangible thing.

j. Your magic is a transforming-stage that goes from 'feeling' (need, want and desire), into 'touch' (touch, contact and grasp). From a mind to a body **"How and why does this happen? "** .. The body creates a 'touch' for what the body and nerves 'feel', which is derived from what the mind is holding in place, another way of understanding this is the heart creates a specific beat to match the template of the mind, and sends that wave and vibration rippling throughout the nerves and cells of the body in order to become a physicalized thing. **ELABORATION -** Recognize and realize the hidden principles at play, and figure out the sacred formula to the process in order to do it at will, when wanted, granted/requested.

k. The body is not just a "body" (the word itself doesn't describe/explain anything about its operations, functions/capabilities), it is a magical-manifesting-machine **"What do you mean by 'a magical manifesting machine'? ..** You drink 'juice' of a certain color and turn it into urine of a different color/clear liquid, you eat fruit/vegetable of a certain color, and turn it into 'feces' of a different color, form, and texture. From the entrance of the mouth, to the exit of the sex organ and anus, as the substance goes through the body (from the mouth cavity to the esophagus to the intestine to the stomach to the rectum and urethra), it goes through the principles of consumption, conversion and transformation (along with other principles).

ELABORATION – Anything created and/moving through dark matter or dark cavity or a dark container (the dark container being the inside of the body) goes through energy conversion and energy transformation. The more darkened and concealed the container is, the more conversion and transformation conducts and produces, until it is exited or finds exit.